AMERICA'S FAVORITE BRAND NAME

100 BEST
CHICKEN
RECIPES

Publications International, Ltd.
Favorite Brand Name Recipes at www.fbnr.com

Microwave Cooking: Microwave ovens vary in wattage. Use the cooking times as guidelines and check for doneness before adding more time.

Preparation/Cooking Times: Preparation times are based on the approximate amount of time required to assemble the recipe before cooking, baking, chilling or serving. These times include preparation steps such as measuring, chopping and mixing. The fact that some preparations and cooking can be done simultaneously is taken into account. Preparation of optional ingredients and serving suggestions is not included.

AMERICA'S FAVORITE BRAND NAME

100 BEST CHICKEN RECIPES

100 BEST
Chicken Recipes

Hot & Spicy Buffalo Chicken Wings

Prep Time: *5 minutes*
Cook Time: *35 minutes*

**1 can (15 ounces) DEL MONTE®
    Original Sloppy Joe Sauce
¼ cup thick and chunky salsa,
    medium
1 tablespoon red wine vinegar or
    cider vinegar
20 chicken wings
    (about 4 pounds)**

1. Preheat oven to 400°F.

2. Combine sloppy joe sauce, salsa and vinegar in small bowl. Remove ¼ cup sauce mixture to serve with cooked chicken wings; cover and refrigerate. Set aside remaining sauce mixture.

3. Arrange wings in single layer in large, shallow baking pan; brush wings with sauce mixture.

4. Bake chicken, uncovered, on middle rack in oven 35 minutes or until chicken is no longer pink in center, turning and brushing with remaining sauce mixture after 15 minutes. Serve with reserved ¼ cup sauce. Garnish, if desired. *Makes 4 servings*

Taco Chicken Nachos

- **2 small boneless skinless chicken breasts (about 8 ounces)**
- **1 tablespoon plus 1½ teaspoons taco seasoning mix**
- **1 teaspoon olive oil**
- **¾ cup nonfat sour cream**
- **1 can (4 ounces) chopped mild green chilies, drained**
- **¼ cup minced red onion**
- **1 bag (8 ounces) baked nonfat tortilla chips**
- **1 cup (4 ounces) shredded reduced-fat Cheddar or Monterey Jack cheese**
- **½ cup chopped tomato**
- **¼ cup pitted ripe olive slices (optional)**
- **2 tablespoons chopped fresh cilantro (optional)**

1. Bring 2 cups water to boil in small saucepan. Add chicken. Reduce heat to low; cover. Simmer 10 minutes or until chicken is no longer pink in center. Remove from saucepan; cool. Chop chicken.

2. Combine taco seasoning mix and oil in small bowl; mix until smooth paste forms. Stir in sour cream. Add chicken, green chilies and onion; mix well.

3. Preheat broiler. Arrange tortilla chips on baking sheet; cover chips with chicken mixture and cheese. Broil, 4 inches from heat, 2 to 3 minutes or until chicken mixture is hot and cheese is melted. Sprinkle evenly with tomato, olives, and cilantro, if desired.

Makes 12 servings

Buffalo Bar-B-Q Nuggets

Prep Time: 10 minutes
Marinate Time: 20 minutes
Cook Time: 10 minutes

- **½ cup Frank's® RedHot® Sauce**
- **⅓ cup butter, melted**
- **1½ pounds boneless skinless chicken thighs or breasts**
  Lettuce leaves
  Blue cheese salad dressing (optional)

1. Combine **RedHot** Sauce and butter in small bowl; mix well. Reserve ⅓ cup sauce mixture. Pour remaining sauce over chicken. Cover; refrigerate 20 minutes. Prepare grill.

2. Discard remaining chicken marinade. Place chicken on oiled grid. Grill, over medium coals, about 10 minutes or until no longer pink in center. Heat reserved sauce. Cut chicken into bite-size pieces; toss chicken pieces in warmed sauce.

3. Arrange chicken on lettuce-lined serving platter. Serve with blue cheese dressing, if desired.

Makes 6 to 8 servings

Taco Chicken Nachos

Party Chicken Tarts

2 tablespoons butter or
   margarine
1 cup chopped fresh mushrooms
¼ cup finely chopped celery
¼ cup finely chopped onion
2 tablespoons all-purpose flour
1½ cups chopped cooked chicken
6 tablespoons sour cream
½ teaspoon garlic salt
1 package (10 ounces) flaky
   refrigerator biscuits (10 to
   12 count)
   Vegetable cooking spray
1 tablespoon butter or
   margarine, melted
   Grated Parmesan cheese

Melt 2 tablespoons butter in large
skillet until hot. Add mushrooms, celery
and onion; cook and stir 4 to
5 minutes. Sprinkle with flour; stir in
chicken and sour cream. Cook until
thoroughly heated. Stir in garlic salt;
set aside. Cut each biscuit into
quarters; press each piece into
miniature muffin tins coated with
cooking spray to form tart shell. Brush
each piece with melted butter. Bake
at 400°F 6 minutes. Remove from
oven; reduce oven temperature to
350°F. Fill each tart with 1 teaspoon
chicken mixture; sprinkle with cheese.
Bake 14 to 15 minutes more. Serve
immediately.

Makes 40 to 48 appetizers

Note: For ease in serving at party
time, prepare filling ahead and cook
tarts 5 minutes. Fill and bake just
before serving for best flavor.

Favorite recipe from **National Broiler Council**

Sticky Wings

24 chicken wings (about
   4 pounds)
¾ cup WISH-BONE® Italian
   Dressing*
1 cup apricot or peach
   preserves
1 tablespoon hot pepper sauce
   (optional)**

*Also terrific with WISH-BONE® Robusto Italian or
Just 2 Good Dressing.*

**Use more or less to taste desired.*

Cut tips off chicken wings (save tips
for soup). Cut chicken wings in half at
joint.

For marinade, blend Italian dressing,
preserves and hot pepper sauce. In
large, shallow nonaluminum baking
dish or plastic bag, pour ½ of the
marinade over chicken wings; toss to
coat. Cover, or close bag, and
marinate in refrigerator, turning
occasionally, 3 to 24 hours. Refrigerate
remaining marinade.

Remove wings, discarding marinade.
Grill or broil wings, turning once and
brushing frequently with refrigerated
marinade, until wings are done.

Makes 48 appetizers

Ranch Buffalo Wings

½ cup butter or margarine, melted
¼ cup hot pepper sauce
3 tablespoons vinegar
24 chicken wing drumettes
1 package (1 ounce) HIDDEN VALLEY® Milk Recipe Original Ranch® Salad Dressing Mix
½ teaspoon paprika
1 cup prepared HIDDEN VALLEY® Original Ranch® Salad Dressing
Celery sticks

Preheat oven to 350°F. In small bowl, whisk together butter, pepper sauce and vinegar. Dip drumettes into butter mixture; arrange in single layer in large baking pan. Sprinkle with 1 package salad dressing mix. Bake 30 to 40 minutes or until chicken is browned and juices run clear. Sprinkle with paprika. Serve with prepared salad dressing and celery sticks.

Makes 6 to 8 servings

Red Hot Pepper Wings

28 chicken wing drumettes (2¼ to 3 pounds)
2 tablespoons olive oil
Salt and black pepper
2 tablespoons melted butter
1 teaspoon sugar
¼ to ½ cup hot pepper sauce

Brush chicken with oil; sprinkle with salt and pepper. Grill chicken on covered grill over medium KINGSFORD® Briquets

about 20 minutes until juices run clear, turning every 5 minutes. Combine butter, sugar and pepper sauce in large bowl; add chicken and toss to coat. Serve hot or cold.

Makes 7 servings

Curried Buffalo Wings

15 chicken wings (about 3 pounds)
¼ cup I CAN'T BELIEVE IT'S NOT BUTTER!® Spread
1 tablespoon mild or hot curry powder
2 teaspoons chopped garlic
1 teaspoon salt

Preheat oven to 450°F.

Cut tips off chicken wings (save tips for soup). Cut chicken wings in half at joint; set aside.

In 12-inch skillet, melt I Can't Believe It's Not Butter! Spread over medium heat and cook curry, garlic and salt, stirring frequently, 30 seconds or until curry darkens slightly; set aside.

In bottom of broiler pan, without rack, pour curry sauce over chicken wings and toss to coat. Bake 35 minutes or until chicken wings are golden brown and fully cooked.

Makes 30 appetizers

Coconut Chicken Tenders with Spicy Mango Salsa

1 firm ripe mango, peeled, seeded and chopped
½ cup chopped red bell pepper
3 tablespoons chopped green onion
2 tablespoons chopped fresh cilantro
Salt
Dash ground red pepper
1½ cups flaked coconut
1 egg
1 tablespoon vegetable oil
¾ pound chicken tenders

Combine mango, bell pepper, onion and cilantro in small bowl.

Season to taste with salt and ground red pepper. Transfer half of salsa to food processor; process until finely chopped (almost puréed). Combine with remaining salsa.

Preheat oven to 400°F. Spread coconut on large baking sheet. Bake 5 to 6 minutes or until lightly browned, stirring every 2 minutes. Transfer coconut to food processor; process until finely chopped but not pasty.

Beat egg with oil, salt and red pepper in small bowl. Add chicken tenders; toss to coat. Roll tenders in coconut; arrange on foil-lined baking sheet. Bake 18 to 20 minutes or until no longer pink in center. Serve with spicy mango salsa.

Makes 5 to 6 servings

Buffalo Chicken Wings

24 chicken wings
1 teaspoon salt
¼ teaspoon ground black pepper
4 cups vegetable oil for frying
¼ cup butter or margarine
¼ cup hot pepper sauce
1 teaspoon white wine vinegar
Celery sticks
1 bottle (8 ounces) blue cheese dressing

Cut tips off wings at first joint; discard tips. Cut remaining wings into two parts at the joint; sprinkle with salt and pepper. Heat oil in deep fryer or heavy saucepan to 375°F. Add half the wings; fry about 10 minutes or until golden brown and crisp, stirring occasionally. Remove with slotted spoon; drain on paper towels. Repeat with remaining wings.

Melt butter in small saucepan over medium heat; stir in pepper sauce and vinegar. Cook until thoroughly heated. Place wings on large platter. Pour sauce over wings. Serve warm with celery and dressing for dipping.

Makes 24 appetizers

Favorite recipe from **National Chicken Council**

Buffalo Chicken Wings

Garlicky Gilroy Chicken Wings

2 heads fresh garlic, separated into cloves and peeled
1 cup olive oil, divided
1 teaspoon hot pepper sauce
1 cup grated Parmesan cheese
1 cup Italian-style bread crumbs
1 teaspoon black pepper
2 pounds chicken wings

Place garlic, 1 cup oil and hot pepper sauce in food processor; cover and process until smooth. Pour garlic mixture into bowl. Combine cheese, bread crumbs and pepper in shallow dish. Dip wings, one at a time, into garlic mixture, then roll in crumb mixture, coating evenly.

Grease 13×9-inch nonstick baking pan; arrange wings in single layer in pan. Drizzle remaining garlic mixture over wings; sprinkle with remaining crumb mixture. Bake 45 to 60 minutes or until wings are brown and crisp.

Makes about 6 servings

Sunshine Chicken Drumsticks

½ cup A.1.® Steak Sauce
¼ cup ketchup
¼ cup apricot preserves
12 chicken drumsticks (about 2½ pounds)

Blend steak sauce, ketchup and preserves in small bowl with wire whisk until smooth.

Brush chicken with sauce.

Grill chicken over medium heat for 20 minutes or until no longer pink, turning and brushing with remaining sauce. (Do not baste during last 5 minutes of grilling.) Serve hot.

Makes 12 appetizers

Spicy Wings

16 chicken wings
½ cup olive or vegetable oil
¼ cup balsamic vinegar
¼ cup honey
2 tablespoons brown sugar
2 tablespoons cane syrup or dark corn syrup
1 tablespoon TABASCO® brand Pepper Sauce
½ teaspoon dried thyme leaves
1 teaspoon soy sauce
¼ teaspoon Worcestershire sauce
¼ teaspoon ground nutmeg

Cut off and discard bony wing tips. Cut remaining wings in half. Combine remaining ingredients in large bowl until well blended; add wings. Cover and marinate in refrigerator 1 hour.

Prepare grill. Place wings on grid. Grill 15 to 20 minutes over medium coals, turning frequently.

Makes 32 appetizers

Sunshine Chicken Drumsticks

Pesto Chicken Brushetta

2 tablespoons olive oil, divided
1 teaspoon coarsely chopped garlic, divided
8 diagonal slices (¼ inch thick) sourdough bread, divided
½ cup (2 ounces) grated BELGIOIOSO® Asiago Cheese, divided
2 tablespoons prepared pesto
¼ teaspoon pepper
4 boneless skinless chicken breast halves
12 slices (¼ inch thick) BELGIOIOSO® Fresh Mozzarella Cheese (8 ounces)
2 tomatoes, each cut into 4 slices

In 10-inch skillet, heat 1 tablespoon olive oil and ½ teaspoon garlic. Add 4 slices bread. Cook over medium-high heat, turning once, 5 to 7 minutes or until toasted. Remove from pan. Add remaining 1 tablespoon oil and ½ teaspoon garlic; repeat with remaining bread slices. Sprinkle ¼ cup BelGioioso Asiago Cheese on bread. In same skillet, combine pesto and pepper. Add chicken, coating with pesto. Cook over medium-high heat, turning once, 8 to 10 minutes or until chicken is brown. Place 3 slices BelGioioso Fresh Mozzarella Cheese on each bread slice; top with tomato slice. Slice chicken pieces in half horizontally. Place on tomato; sprinkle with remaining BelGioioso Asiago Cheese. *Makes 4 servings*

Almond Chicken Cups

Prep and Cook Time: 30 minutes

1 tablespoon vegetable oil
½ cup chopped red bell pepper
½ cup chopped onion
2 cups chopped cooked chicken
⅔ cup prepared sweet-sour sauce
½ cup chopped almonds
2 tablespoons soy sauce
6 (6- or 7-inch) flour tortillas

1. Preheat oven to 400°F. Heat oil in small skillet over medium heat until hot. Add bell pepper and onion. Cook and stir 3 minutes or until crisp-tender.

2. Combine vegetable mixture, chicken, sweet-sour sauce, almonds and soy sauce in medium bowl; mix until well blended.

3. Cut each tortilla in half. Place each half in 2¾-inch muffin cup. Fill each with about ¼ cup chicken mixture.

4. Bake 8 to 10 minutes or until tortilla edges are crisp and filling is hot. Remove muffin pan to cooling rack. Let stand 5 minutes before serving.
Makes 12 chicken cups

Almond Chicken Cups

Almond Chicken Kabobs

⅓ cup A.1.® BOLD & SPICY Steak Sauce
1 tablespoon GREY POUPON® Dijon Mustard
1 tablespoon honey
1 tablespoon vegetable oil
1 tablespoon lemon juice
1 clove garlic, crushed
4 boneless skinless chicken breast halves (about 1 pound)
¼ cup toasted slivered almonds, finely chopped

Blend steak sauce, mustard, honey, oil, lemon juice and garlic; set aside.

Cut each chicken breast half into 8 cubes. Combine chicken cubes and ½ cup steak sauce mixture in nonmetal bowl. Cover; refrigerate 1 hour, turning occasionally.

Soak 16 (10-inch) wooden skewers in water for at least 30 minutes. Thread 2 chicken cubes onto each skewer. Grill kabobs over medium heat for 6 to 8 minutes or until done, turning and brushing with remaining sauce. Remove from grill; quickly roll kabobs in almonds. Serve immediately.

Makes 16 appetizers

Hot & Cool Teriyaki Wings

4 pounds chicken wings (about 20 wings)
¾ cup KIKKOMAN® Teriyaki Marinade & Sauce
2 teaspoons crushed red pepper
¾ teaspoon hot pepper sauce
Cool Teriyaki Dipping Sauce (recipe follows)

Discard chicken wing tips (or save for stock); place wings in large plastic food storage bag. Combine teriyaki sauce, crushed red pepper and pepper sauce; pour over wings. Press air out of bag; close top securely. Turn bag over several times to coat all pieces well. Refrigerate 8 hours or overnight. Remove wings; place on grill 4 to 5 inches from hot coals. Cook 20 to 25 minutes, or until tender, turning over frequently. (Or, place on rack of broiler pan. Broil 4 to 5 inches from heat 20 to 25 minutes, or until tender, turning over frequently.) Meanwhile, prepare Cool Teriyaki Dipping Sauce. Serve with wings.

Makes 4 servings

Cool Teriyaki Dipping Sauce:
Combine ¾ cup sour cream, ⅓ cup mayonnaise, 1 tablespoon *each* minced green onions, minced fresh parsley and Kikkoman Teriyaki Sauce. Refrigerate until ready to serve.

Almond Chicken Kabobs

Party Chicken Sandwiches

Prep: *10 minutes*
Broil: *5 minutes*

1½ **cups finely chopped cooked chicken**
1 **cup MIRACLE WHIP® or MIRACLE WHIP LIGHT Dressing**
1 **can (4 ounces) chopped green chilies, drained**
¾ **cup (3 ounces) KRAFT® Shredded Sharp Cheddar Cheese**
¼ **cup finely chopped onion**
36 **party rye or pumpernickel bread slices**

HEAT broiler.

MIX chicken, dressing, chilies, cheese and onions. Spread evenly onto bread slices.

BROIL 5 minutes or until lightly browned. Serve hot.

Makes 3 dozen

Make-Ahead: Prepare chicken mixture as directed; cover. Refrigerate. When ready to serve, spread bread with chicken mixture. Broil as directed.

Sesame Chicken Nuggets

2 **tablespoons sesame seeds**
1 **tablespoon Worcestershire sauce**
1 **tablespoon water**
1 **teaspoon granulated sugar**
1 **teaspoon chili powder**
¼ **teaspoon garlic powder**
1 **pound boneless chicken breasts, skinned and cut into 1-inch cubes**
Barbecue Sauce (recipe follows)

In small bowl, combine all ingredients except chicken and Barbecue Sauce; mix well. Add chicken and coat evenly. Spread on broiling pan. Broil 10 minutes or until lightly browned, turning once. Serve with Barbecue Sauce or stuff into pita pockets with lettuce and sliced tomato.

Note: This recipe can be doubled for an easy dinner dish. Serve any leftover chicken nuggets in pita pocket sandwiches.

BARBECUE SAUCE:

1 **can (8 ounces) tomato sauce**
1 **teaspoon granulated sugar**
1 **teaspoon red wine vinegar**
½ **teaspoon Worcestershire sauce**
½ **teaspoon chili powder**
¼ **teaspoon garlic powder**

In medium saucepan combine all ingredients; simmer 15 minutes, stirring occasionally. Use as a dipping sauce for chicken nuggets. *Makes 1 cup*

Favorite recipe from **The Sugar Association, Inc.**

Tortilla Crunch Chicken Fingers

1 envelope LIPTON® RECIPE SECRETS® Savory Herb with Garlic Soup Mix
1 cup finely crushed plain tortilla chips or cornflakes (about 3 ounces)
1½ pounds boneless, skinless chicken breasts, cut into strips
1 egg
2 tablespoons water
2 tablespoons margarine or butter, melted

Preheat oven to 400°F.

In medium bowl, combine Savory Herb with Garlic soup mix and tortilla chips. In large plastic bag or bowl, combine chicken and egg beaten with water until evenly coated. Remove chicken and dip in tortilla mixture until evenly coated; discard bag. On 15½×10½×1-inch jelly-roll pan sprayed with nonstick cooking spray, arrange chicken; drizzle with margarine. Bake, uncovered, 12 minutes or until chicken is done.
Makes about 24 chicken fingers

Tip: Serve chicken with your favorite fresh or prepared salsa.

Sweet & Spicy Drumettes

1¾ cups (16-ounce jar) ORTEGA® Green Chile Picante Sauce, medium, divided
⅓ cup honey
¼ cup soy sauce
¼ cup Dijon mustard
2 pounds (about 20) chicken wing drumettes

COMBINE 1 cup picante sauce, honey, soy sauce and mustard in large bowl or in large resealable plastic food-storage bag.

ADD drumettes; toss to coat well. Marinate in refrigerator for at least 2 hours.

PLACE chicken on greased or foil-lined baking pan. Bake in preheated 375°F oven for 30 to 35 minutes or until no longer pink near bone. Serve with remaining ¾ cup picante sauce for dipping.   *Makes 20 appetizers*

Ginger Wings with Peach Dipping Sauce

Peach Dipping Sauce (recipe follows)
2 pounds chicken wings
¼ cup soy sauce
2 cloves garlic, minced
1 teaspoon ground ginger
¼ teaspoon white pepper

1. Preheat oven to 400°F. Line 15×10×1-inch jelly roll pan with foil; set aside. Prepare Peach Dipping Sauce; set aside.

2. Cut off and discard wing tips from chicken. Cut each wing in half at joint. Combine soy sauce, garlic, ginger and pepper in large bowl. Add chicken and stir until well coated. Place chicken in single layer in prepared pan. Bake 40 to 50 minutes or until browned, turning over halfway through cooking time. Serve hot with Peach Dipping Sauce.

Makes 6 appetizer servings

Peach Dipping Sauce

½ cup peach preserves
2 tablespoons light corn syrup
1 teaspoon white vinegar
¼ teaspoon ground ginger
¾ teaspoon soy sauce

Combine preserves, corn syrup, vinegar and ginger in small saucepan. Cook and stir over medium-high heat until mixture simmers. Remove from heat; add soy sauce. Let cool.

Makes ½ cup

Gorgonzola Buffalo Wings

Dressing
¼ cup mayonnaise
3 tablespoons sour cream
1½ tablespoons white wine vinegar
¼ teaspoon sugar
⅓ cup (1½ ounces) BELGIOIOSO® Gorgonzola

Chicken
2 pounds chicken wings
3 tablespoons hot pepper sauce
1 tablespoon vegetable oil
1 clove garlic, minced

For dressing
Combine mayonnaise, sour cream, vinegar and sugar in small bowl. Stir in BelGioioso Gorgonzola; cover and refrigerate until serving.

For chicken
Place chicken in large resealable plastic food storage bag. Combine pepper sauce, oil and garlic in separate small bowl; pour over chicken. Seal bag tightly; turn to coat. Marinate in refrigerator at least 1 hour or, for hotter flavor, up to 24 hours, turning occasionally.

Prepare grill. Drain chicken, discarding marinade. Place chicken on grill. Grill on covered grill over medium-hot coals or until chicken is no longer pink, turning 3-4 times. Serve with dressing.

Makes 4 servings

Ginger Wings with Peach Dipping Sauce

100 BEST
Chicken Recipes

SUPER SOUPS, STEWS & SALADS

Country Chicken Stew

Prep Time: 5 minutes
Cook Time: 20 minutes

2 tablespoons butter or margarine
1 pound boneless skinless chicken breasts, cut into 1-inch cubes
½ pound small red potatoes, cut into ½-inch cubes
2 tablespoons cooking sherry
2 jars (12 ounces each) golden chicken gravy
1 bag (16 ounces) BIRDS EYE® frozen Farm Fresh Mixtures Broccoli, Green Beans, Pearl Onions and Red Peppers
½ cup water

• Melt butter in large saucepan over high heat. Add chicken and potatoes; cook about 8 minutes or until browned, stirring frequently.

• Add sherry; cook until evaporated. Add gravy, vegetables and water.

• Bring to boil; reduce heat to medium-low. Cover and cook 5 minutes. *Makes 4 to 6 servings*

24

Southwestern Chicken Soup

Prep Time: *10 minutes*
Cook Time: *22 minutes*

½ **teaspoon salt**
¼ **teaspoon garlic powder**
¼ **teaspoon black pepper**
1 **pound boneless skinless chicken breast halves (1 pound)**
1 **tablespoon olive oil**
1 **medium onion, halved and sliced**
1 **small hot chili pepper,* seeded and chopped (optional)**
4 **cans (about 14 ounces each) fat-free reduced-sodium chicken broth**
2 **cups peeled and diced potatoes**
2 **small zucchini, sliced**
1½ **cups frozen corn**
1 **cup diced tomato**
1 **tablespoon chopped fresh cilantro**
2 **tablespoons lime or lemon juice**

*Hot chili peppers can sting and irritate the skin; wear rubber gloves when handling peppers and do not touch eyes. Wash hands after handling.

1. Combine salt, garlic powder and pepper in small bowl; sprinkle evenly over chicken.

2. Heat oil in Dutch oven over medium-high heat. Add chicken; cook, without stirring, 2 minutes or until golden. Turn chicken and cook 2 minutes more. Add onion and pepper; if desired; cook 2 minutes longer, adding a little chicken broth if needed to prevent burning.

3. Add chicken broth; bring to a boil. Stir in potatoes. Reduce heat to low; cook 5 minutes. Add zucchini, corn and tomato; cook 10 minutes longer or until vegetables are tender. Just before serving, stir in cilantro and lime juice.   *Makes 6 servings*

Salsa Corn Soup with Chicken

3 **quarts chicken broth**
2 **pounds boneless skinless chicken breasts, cooked and diced**
2 **packages (10 ounces each) frozen whole kernel corn, thawed**
4 **jars (11 ounces each) NEWMAN'S OWN® All Natural Salsa**
4 **large carrots, diced**

Bring chicken broth to a boil in Dutch oven. Add chicken, corn, Newman's Own® Salsa and carrots. Bring to a boil. Reduce heat and simmer until carrots are tender.

Makes 8 servings

Southwestern Chicken Soup

Tomato Chicken Gumbo

Prep and Cook Time: *1 hour*

6 chicken thighs
½ pound hot sausage links or Polish sausage, sliced
3 cups water
1 can (14 ounces) chicken broth
½ cup uncooked long-grain white rice
1 can (26 ounces) DEL MONTE® Traditional or Chunky Garlic and Herb Spaghetti Sauce
1 can (11 ounces) DEL MONTE SUMMER CRISP™ Whole Kernel Golden Sweet Corn, drained
1 medium green bell pepper, diced

1. Preheat oven to 400°F. In large shallow baking pan, place chicken and sausage. Bake 35 minutes or until chicken is no longer pink in center. Cool slightly.

2. Remove skin from chicken; cut meat into cubes. Cut sausage into slices ½ inch thick.

3. Bring water and broth to boil in 6-quart pot. Add chicken, sausage and rice. Cover; cook over medium heat 15 minutes.

4. Stir in remaining ingredients; bring to boil. Cover; cook 5 minutes or until rice is tender.   *Makes 4 servings*

Tip: Add additional water or broth for a thinner gumbo. For spicier gumbo, serve with hot red pepper sauce.

Tomato Chicken Gumbo

Pantry Soup

½ cup dry pasta (rotini or rotelle), cooked and drained
2 teaspoons olive oil
8 ounces boneless skinless chicken, cubed
2 cans (14.5 ounces each) CONTADINA® Diced Tomatoes with Italian Herbs, undrained
¾ cup chicken broth
¾ cup water
1 cup garbanzo beans, undrained
1 cup kidney beans, undrained
1 package (16 ounces) frozen mixed vegetables
2 teaspoons lemon juice

1. Heat oil in 5-quart saucepan with lid; sauté chicken about 3 to 4 minutes or until cooked, stirring occasionally.

2. Mix in tomatoes, broth, water, garbanzo and kidney beans; cover and bring to a boil. Add mixed vegetables and pasta; bring to boil.

3. Reduce heat; cover and simmer 3 minutes or until vegetables are tender. Stir in lemon juice; serve with condiments, if desired.
Makes 6 to 8 servings

Optional Condiments: Grated Parmesan cheese, chopped fresh basil or parsley, or croutons.

Chicken Curry Soup

6 ounces boneless skinless chicken breast, cut into ½-inch pieces
3½ teaspoons curry powder, divided
1 teaspoon olive oil
¾ cup chopped apple
½ cup sliced carrot
⅓ cup sliced celery
¼ teaspoon ground cloves
2 cans (about 14 ounces each) fat-free reduced-sodium chicken broth
½ cup orange juice
4 ounces uncooked radiatore pasta

1. Coat chicken with 3 teaspoons curry powder. Heat oil in large saucepan over medium heat until hot. Add chicken; cook and stir 3 minutes or until no longer pink in center. Remove from pan; set aside.

2. Add apple, carrot, celery, remaining ½ teaspoon curry powder and cloves to same pan; cook, stirring occasionally, 5 minutes. Add chicken broth and juice; bring to a boil over high heat. Reduce heat to medium-low. Add pasta; cover. Cook, stirring occasionally, 8 to 10 minutes or until pasta is tender; add chicken. Remove from heat. Ladle into soup tureen or individual bowls. Top each serving with a dollop of plain nonfat yogurt, if desired. *Makes 4 (¾-cup) servings*

Cajun-Style Chicken Soup

1½ **pounds chicken thighs**
4 **cups chicken broth**
1 **can (8 ounces) tomato sauce**
2 **ribs celery, sliced**
1 **medium onion, chopped**
2 **cloves garlic, minced**
2 **bay leaves**
1 to 1½ **teaspoons salt**
½ **teaspoon ground cumin**
¼ **teaspoon paprika**
¼ **teaspoon ground red pepper**
¼ **teaspoon black pepper**
   Dash white pepper
1 **large green bell pepper, chopped**
⅓ **cup uncooked rice**
8 **ounces fresh or frozen okra, cut into ½-inch slices**
   Hot pepper sauce (optional)

Place chicken, chicken broth, tomato sauce, celery, onion, garlic, bay leaves, salt, cumin, paprika, red pepper, black pepper, and white pepper in 5-quart Dutch oven. Bring to a boil over high heat. Reduce heat to medium-low; simmer, uncovered, 1 hour or until chicken is tender, skimming foam that rises to the surface.

Remove chicken from soup; cool slightly. Skim fat from soup. Remove chicken meat from bones; discard skin and bones. Cut chicken into bite-size pieces.

Add chicken, bell pepper and rice to soup. Bring to a boil. Reduce heat; simmer, uncovered, about 12 minutes

or until rice is tender. Add okra; simmer an additional 8 minutes or until okra is tender. Discard bay leaves. Ladle soup into bowls; serve with hot pepper sauce, if desired.

Makes 6 servings

Campbell's® Hearty Chicken Noodle Soup

Prep/Cook Time: 20 minutes

2 **cans (10½ ounces each) CAMPBELL'S® Condensed Chicken Broth**
1 **cup water**
   Generous dash pepper
1 **medium carrot, sliced (about ½ cup)**
1 **stalk celery, sliced (about ½ cup)**
2 **skinless, boneless chicken breast halves, cut up**
½ **cup** *uncooked* **medium egg noodles**

1. In medium saucepan mix broth, water, pepper, carrot, celery and chicken. Over medium-high heat, heat to a boil.

2. Stir in noodles. Reduce heat to medium. Cook 10 minutes or until noodles are done, stirring often.

Makes 4 servings

Tip: Save time by using precut carrots and celery from your supermarket salad bar.

Cajun-Style Chicken Soup

Cobb Salad with Tarragon Dressing

Prep Time: *45 minutes*

TARRAGON DRESSING
- 1 cup plain yogurt
- ½ cup reduced-fat mayonnaise
- ½ cup chopped fresh parsley
- 4 tablespoons chopped fresh tarragon *or* 1 tablespoon dried tarragon leaves
- ¼ cup milk
- 3 tablespoons *Frank's® RedHot®* Sauce
- 2 tablespoons lime juice
- 2 teaspoons honey

SALAD
- 8 cups thinly sliced Romaine lettuce
- 2 cups (10 ounces) chopped cooked chicken
- 6 slices crisply cooked bacon, crumbled
- 3 hard cooked eggs, cut into wedges
- 4 plum tomatoes, diced
- 1 can (8¼ ounces) sliced beets, drained and cut into strips
- 1 small ripe avocado, diced
- 1 small red onion, diced
- 1½ cups diced seeded cucumber
- ½ cup (2 ounces) crumbled Gorgonzola cheese

1. Combine dressing ingredients in medium bowl; mix until well blended.

2. Arrange lettuce on serving platter or in 8 individual salad bowls. Arrange chicken, bacon, eggs, tomatoes, beets, avocado, onion, cucumber and Gorgonzola in mounds or rows over lettuce. Serve with Tarragon Dressing.

Makes 8 servings
(two cups dressing)

BLT Chicken Salad for Two

- 2 boneless skinless chicken breast halves
- ¼ cup mayonnaise or salad dressing
- ½ teaspoon black pepper
- 4 large leaf lettuce leaves
- 1 large tomato, seeded and diced
- 3 slices crisp-cooked bacon, crumbled
- 1 hard-cooked egg, sliced Additional mayonnaise or salad dressing

1. Brush chicken with mayonnaise; sprinkle with pepper. Grill over hot coals 5 to 7 minutes per side or until no longer pink in center. Cool slightly; cut into thin strips.

2. Arrange lettuce leaves on serving plates. Top with chicken, tomato, bacon and egg. Spoon additional mayonnaise over top.

Makes 2 servings

Tropical Chicken Salad

Tropical Salad Dressing (recipe follows)
3 cups cubed cooked chicken
¾ cup coarsely chopped celery
¾ cup seedless red or green grape halves
¾ cup coarsely chopped macadamia nuts or toasted almonds
Lettuce leaves
Strawberries and kiwifruit for garnish
Toasted flaked coconut for garnish*

To toast coconut, spread evenly on cookie sheet. Toast in preheated 350°F oven 7 minutes. Stir and toast 1 to 2 minutes more or until light golden brown.

Prepare Tropical Salad Dressing. Combine chicken, celery, grapes and nuts in large bowl; stir in 1 cup dressing. Cover; refrigerate 1 hour. Mound chicken salad on lettuce-lined platter or individual plates. Garnish with strawberries, kiwifruit and coconut. Serve with remaining dressing. *Makes 4 servings*

Tropical Salad Dressing: Place ½ cup cream of coconut, ⅓ cup red wine vinegar, 1 teaspoon dry mustard, 1 teaspoon salt and 1 clove garlic, peeled, in blender or food processor container. With processor on, slowly add 1 cup vegetable oil in thin stream, processing until smooth.

Black Bean and Mango Chicken Salad

Prep: *10 minutes plus refrigerating*

1 can (16 ounces) black beans, drained, rinsed
1 package (10 ounces) frozen corn, thawed
1 cup chopped ripe mango
½ pound boneless skinless chicken breasts, grilled, cut up
½ cup chopped red pepper
⅓ cup chopped fresh cilantro
⅓ cup chopped red onion
¼ cup lime juice
1 envelope GOOD SEASONS® Italian Salad Dressing Mix

TOSS all ingredients in large bowl. Refrigerate.

SERVE with baked tortilla chips, if desired. *Makes 4 servings*

Black Bean and Mango Chicken Salad

34

Chili-Crusted Grilled Chicken Caesar Salad

1 to 2 lemons
1 tablespoon minced garlic, divided
1½ teaspoons dried oregano leaves, crushed, divided
1 teaspoon chili powder
1 pound boneless skinless chicken breasts
1 tablespoon olive oil
2 anchovy fillets, minced
1 large head romaine lettuce, cut into 1-inch strips
¼ cup grated Parmesan cheese
4 whole wheat rolls

1. Grate lemon peel; measure 1 to 2 teaspoons. Juice lemon; measure ¼ cup. Combine lemon peel and 1 tablespoon juice in small bowl. Set ¼ teaspoon garlic aside. Add remaining garlic, 1 teaspoon oregano and chili powder to lemon peel mixture; stir to combine. Rub chicken with lemon peel mixture.

2. Combine remaining 3 tablespoons lemon juice, ¼ teaspoon garlic, remaining ½ teaspoon oregano, oil and anchovies in large bowl. Add lettuce; toss to coat. Sprinkle with cheese; toss.

3. Spray cold grid with nonstick cooking spray. Prepare grill for direct grilling. Place chicken on grid 3 to 4 inches above medium-hot coals. Grill chicken 5 to 6 minutes. Turn chicken; grill 3 to 4 minutes or until chicken is no longer pink in center.

4. Arrange salad on 4 large plates. Slice chicken. Fan on each salad. Serve with whole wheat rolls.
Makes 4 servings

Blue Cheese Chicken Salad

Prep Time: 10 minutes
Cook Time: 10 minutes

1 can (14½ ounces) DEL MONTE® Diced Tomatoes with Garlic & Onion
½ pound boneless, skinned chicken breasts, cut into strips
½ teaspoon dried tarragon
6 cups torn assorted lettuces
½ medium red onion, thinly sliced
½ medium cucumber, thinly sliced
⅓ cup crumbled blue cheese
¼ cup Italian dressing

1. Drain tomatoes, reserving liquid. In large skillet, cook reserved liquid until thickened, about 5 minutes, stirring occasionally.

2. Add chicken and tarragon; cook until chicken is no longer pink, stirring frequently.

3. Cool. In large bowl, toss chicken and tomato liquid with remaining ingredients. *Makes 4 servings*

Chicken Salad with Goat Cheese

Salad Vinaigrette (recipe follows)
6 cups fresh, mixed salad greens
½ small red onion, thinly sliced
1 small carrot, cut in strips
1 yellow bell pepper, cut in strips
5 ounces goat cheese, cut in 4 pieces
4 small rosemary sprigs (or basil leaves)
4 chicken breasts, halved, boned with skins
Olive oil, as needed
Salt and pepper to taste
¼ cup pine nuts, toasted

Preheat oven broiler. Prepare vinaigrette. In a large bowl combine salad greens, onion, carrot and bell pepper; chill. Push a piece of goat cheese and sprig of rosemary between the skin and meat of each chicken breast. Smooth the skin over the meat. Brush with olive oil; season with salt and pepper.

Place chicken on broiler pan, skin side up. Broil 7 or 8 minutes per side or until breast meat is no longer pink. Toss salad with dressing; divide among 4 small plates. Place each chicken breast on a cutting board; cut into slices. Arrange on a bed of salad. Garnish with pine nuts. Serve at once.
Makes 4 servings

Salad Vinaigrette

⅓ cup olive oil
2 tablespoons balsamic vinegar or red wine vinegar
1 clove garlic, minced
Salt and pepper to taste

Whisk ingredients together.

Favorite recipe from **National Chicken Council**

Chicken Salad

¼ cup mayonnaise
¼ cup sour cream
1 tablespoon lemon juice
1 teaspoon sugar
1 teaspoon grated lemon peel
1 teaspoon Dijon mustard
½ teaspoon salt
⅛ to ¼ teaspoon white pepper
2 cups diced cooked chicken
1 cup sliced celery
¼ cup sliced green onions
Lettuce leaves
Crumbled blue cheese (optional)

Combine mayonnaise, sour cream, lemon juice, sugar, lemon peel, mustard, salt and pepper in large bowl.

Add chicken, celery and green onions; stir to combine. Cover; refrigerate at least 1 hour to allow flavors to blend.

Serve salad on lettuce-lined plate. Sprinkle with blue cheese, if desired.
Makes 4 servings

Balsamic Chicken Salad

Prep Time: *10 minutes*

⅓ **cup olive oil**
¼ **cup** *French's®* **Honey Mustard**
2 **tablespoons balsamic or red wine vinegar**
1 **teaspoon minced shallots or onion**
8 **cups mixed salad greens, washed and torn**
1 **package (10 ounces) fully cooked carved chicken breasts**
1 **package (4 ounces) goat or Feta cheese, crumbled**
1 **cup croutons**

1. Whisk together oil, mustard, vinegar, shallots, *2 tablespoons water* and *⅛ teaspoon salt.*

2. Arrange salad greens, chicken, cheese and croutons on serving plates. Serve with dressing.

Makes 4 servings

California Chef Salad

Prep time: *6 to 8 minutes*
Cook time: *None*

1 **package (10 ounces) PERDUE® SHORT CUTS® Fresh Lemon Pepper Carved Chicken Breast**
½ **cup prepared Catalina-style dressing, divided**
1 **package (10 ounces) prewashed fresh mixed salad greens**
4 **ounces PERDUE® Turkey Ham, cut into strips**
4 **ounces sliced Swiss cheese, cut into strips**
2 **ripe tomatoes, cut into wedges**

Combine chicken with ¼ cup dressing. Place greens on four chilled dinner plates. Arrange chicken slices, ham and cheese over greens. Garnish with tomato wedges. Drizzle with remaining dressing and serve with hot, crusty sourdough rolls.

Makes 4 servings

Tip: Another choice for the salad bowl is PERDUE® Rotisserie Chicken sliced into thin strips.

Balsamic Chicken Salad

DOWN-HOME FAVORITES

Campbell's® Cornbread Chicken Pot Pie

Prep Time: *10 minutes*
Cook Time: *30 minutes*

1 can (10¾ ounces) CAMPBELL'S® Condensed Cream of Chicken Soup *or* 98% Fat Free Cream of Chicken Soup
1 can (about 8 ounces) whole kernel corn, drained
2 cups cubed cooked chicken or turkey
1 package (8½ ounces) corn muffin mix
¾ cup milk
1 egg
½ cup shredded Cheddar cheese (2 ounces)

1. Preheat oven to 400°F. In 9-inch pie plate mix soup, corn and chicken.

2. Mix muffin mix, milk and egg. Pour over chicken mixture. Bake for 30 minutes or until golden. Sprinkle with cheese.   *Makes 4 servings*

Campbell's® Cornbread Chicken Chili Pot Pie: In Step 1 add 1 can (about 4 ounces) chopped green chilies, drained, with the corn.

Noodly Chicken & Green Bean Skillet

Prep Time: 5 minutes
Cook Time: 20 minutes

3 tablespoons margarine or butter, divided
¾ pound boneless, skinless chicken breasts, cut into ¾-inch pieces
1 (2.8-ounce) can French fried real onions (about 2 cups), divided
¾ cup milk
1 (4.7-ounce) package PASTA RONI® Fettuccine Alfredo
1 (14½-ounce) can French-style green beans, drained

1. In large skillet over medium-high heat, melt 1 tablespoon margarine. Add chicken; sauté 5 minutes or until chicken is no longer pink inside. Stir in 1½ cups fried onions. Remove from skillet; set aside.

2. In same skillet, bring 1¼ cups water, milk, remaining 2 tablespoons margarine, pasta and Special Seasonings to a boil. Reduce heat to low. Gently boil uncovered, 4 minutes, stirring occasionally.

3. Stir in chicken mixture and green beans; simmer 1 to 2 minutes or until pasta is tender, stirring frequently. Top with remaining fried onions.

Makes 4 servings

Baked Barbecue Chicken

1 cut-up whole chicken (about 3 pounds)
1 small onion, cut into slices
1½ cups ketchup
½ cup packed brown sugar
¼ cup Worcestershire sauce
2 tablespoons lemon juice
1 tablespoon liquid smoke

Preheat oven to 375°F. Place chicken in 13×9-inch baking dish coated with nonstick cooking spray. Arrange onion slices over top.

Combine ketchup, brown sugar, Worcestershire sauce, lemon juice and liquid smoke in small saucepan. Heat over medium heat 2 to 3 minutes or until sugar dissolves. Pour over chicken.

Bake chicken 1 hour or until juices run clear. Discard onion slices. Let stand 10 minutes before serving.

Makes 6 servings

Serving Suggestion: Serve with baked potatoes, crusty French bread and tossed green salad.

Baked Barbecue Chicken

Creamy Herbed Chicken

1 package (9 ounces) fresh bow-tie pasta or fusilli*
1 tablespoon vegetable oil
2 boneless, skinless chicken breasts, cut into halves, then cut into ½-inch strips
1 small red onion, cut into slices
1 package (10 ounces) frozen green peas, thawed and drained
1 yellow or red bell pepper, cut into strips
½ cup chicken broth
1 container (8 ounces) soft cream cheese with garlic and herbs
Salt and black pepper

Substitute dried bow-tie pasta or fusilli for fresh pasta. Cooking time will be longer; follow package directions.

Cook pasta in lightly salted boiling water according to package directions, about 5 minutes; drain.

Meanwhile, heat oil in large skillet or wok over medium-high heat. Add chicken and onion; cook and stir 3 minutes or until chicken is no longer pink in center. Add peas and bell pepper; cook and stir 4 minutes. Reduce heat to medium.

Stir in broth and cream cheese. Cook, stirring constantly, until cream cheese is melted. Combine pasta and chicken mixture in serving bowl; mix lightly. Season to taste with salt and black pepper. Garnish as desired.
Makes 4 servings

Big Easy Chicken Creole

1 package (about 2½ pounds) PERDUE® Fresh Split Skinless Chicken Breasts
1½ to 2 teaspoons Creole or Cajun seasoning
Salt to taste
2 tablespoons canola oil
½ green bell pepper, seeded and chopped (about ¾ cup)
1 small onion, peeled and chopped (about ¾ cup)
1 can (14½ ounces) Cajun- or Mexican-style tomatoes
¼ cup white wine (optional)
2 tablespoons minced fresh parsley (optional)

With sharp knife, make 3 to 4 parallel slashes in each piece of chicken. Rub with seasoning mixture and salt, getting seasonings into slashes. In large skillet over medium heat, heat oil. Add chicken and cook 5 to 6 minutes per side, until browned. Remove and set aside. Add pepper and onion to skillet; sauté 2 to 3 minutes until softened. Stir in tomatoes and wine. Return chicken to pan, meat-side down. Partially cover with lid and reduce heat to medium-low. Simmer 30 to 35 minutes, until chicken is tender and cooked through (meat thermometer inserted in thickest part of breast should register 170°F). Sprinkle with parsley; serve over hot, fluffy rice. *Makes 4 servings*

Creamy Herbed Chicken

Rocky Mountain Hash with Smoked Chicken

1½ pounds Colorado russet variety potatoes, unpeeled
2 tablespoons olive oil, divided
1 teaspoon salt, divided
¼ teaspoon black pepper
Nonstick cooking spray
2 cups chopped red or yellow onions
2 tablespoons bottled minced garlic
2 cups diced red bell pepper
⅛ to ¼ teaspoon cayenne pepper
2 cups shredded smoked chicken or turkey
1 can (11 ounces) whole kernel corn

Cut potatoes into ½- to ¾-inch chunks. Toss with 1 tablespoon oil, ½ teaspoon salt and black pepper. Spray 15×10×1-inch baking pan with nonstick cooking spray. Arrange potato chunks in single layer; roast at 450°F for 20 to 30 minutes or until tender, stirring and tossing occasionally. In large skillet heat remaining 1 tablespoon oil. Sauté onions and garlic until tender. Add red bell pepper, remaining ½ teaspoon salt and cayenne pepper. Cook and stir until peppers are crisp-tender. Stir in chicken, corn and potatoes. Cook and stir until heated through.

Makes 6 to 8 servings

Favorite recipe from **Colorado Potato Administrative Committee**

Honey Baked Chicken

1 cup dry bread crumbs
3 tablespoons cornmeal
1 tablespoon LAWRY'S® Seasoned Salt
2 teaspoons LAWRY'S® Garlic Powder with Parsley
¼ teaspoon cayenne pepper
3 tablespoons honey
3 tablespoons Dijon-style mustard
2 tablespoons water
2½ to 3 pounds chicken fryer pieces

In medium bowl, combine bread crumbs, cornmeal, Seasoned Salt, Garlic Powder with Parsley and cayenne pepper; mix well and set aside. In small bowl, combine honey, mustard and water; mix well. Dip chicken pieces in honey mixture then in bread crumbs. Place in 13×9×2-inch baking dish. Bake, uncovered, in 375°F oven 45 to 50 minutes until chicken is no longer pink in center and juices run clear when cut (175°-180°F at thickest joint).

Makes 6 to 8 servings

Serving Suggestion: Serve with steamed carrots and peas or broccoli and mushrooms.

Baked Chicken with Crispy Cheese-Garlic Crust

1 teaspoon olive oil
½ cup chopped garlic (one large head)
4 tablespoons water, divided
½ cup dry bread crumbs
¼ cup Dijon mustard (or more to taste)
1 cup (4 ounces) shredded JARLSBERG Cheese
3 pounds chicken pieces, skin removed and trimmed of fat

Preheat oven to 400°F. Heat oil in large skillet over high heat. Add garlic; cook and stir 2 minutes. Add 2 tablespoons water; cover tightly. Reduce heat to low; cook 4 minutes.

Meanwhile, mix crumbs and mustard. Add garlic and blend well. Add cheese plus remaining 2 tablespoons water and mix to make a paste.

Arrange chicken on rack in foil-lined baking pan. Pat thin layer of garlic-cheese paste on top side of chicken pieces to form a crust. Bake, loosely tented with foil, 1 hour or until juices run clear when pierced with a knife.

Makes 3 to 4 servings

Kahlúa® Stir-Fry Chicken

1½ pounds boneless skinless chicken, cut into ½-inch pieces
2 tablespoons beaten egg
¼ cup plus 2 tablespoons vegetable oil, divided
2 tablespoons plus 1 teaspoon cornstarch, divided
½ cup water chestnuts, sliced
6 asparagus tips, fresh or frozen
1 green bell pepper, cut into ½-inch strips
4 ounces mushrooms, sliced
4 ounces snow peas
3 tablespoons KAHLÚA® Liqueur
1 cup cashews
3 green onions, chopped

Coat chicken in mixture of egg, 2 tablespoons oil and 2 tablespoons cornstarch. Heat remaining ¼ cup oil in wok or skillet. Add chicken. Cook until golden brown; remove and drain well. Remove all but 2 tablespoons oil from wok; heat. Add all vegetables except green onions. Stir-fry 3 to 5 minutes. Combine Kahlúa® and remaining 1 teaspoon cornstarch; add to vegetables. Bring to a boil, then simmer to slightly thicken. Add chicken and cashews; heat thoroughly. Remove to serving platter. Garnish with green onions.

Makes 4 to 6 servings

47

Old-Fashioned Chicken Fricassee

1 PERDUE® Fresh OVEN STUFFER® Roaster Breast (about 2¾ pounds)
1 can (49½ ounces) chicken broth
2 cups fresh or frozen baby carrots
1 cup frozen pearl onions
¼ cup heavy cream or half-and-half
¼ cup flour
Salt and pepper to taste
½ to 1 teaspoon fresh lemon juice

Place breast in large Dutch oven or pot; add chicken broth, carrots and onions. Over medium heat, bring to a simmer. Poach chicken, uncovered, 60 to 70 minutes or until cooked through, skimming off any foam that rises to top of broth. Add water, if necessary, so that breast is always covered with liquid.

Remove chicken and set aside until cool enough to handle. Pour broth and vegetables into colander set over bowl. Reserve vegetables and broth. Wash Dutch oven. Remove and dice meat from chicken breast; discard skin and bones.

Return 3½ cups broth to clean Dutch oven; reserve any remaining broth for another use. In large measuring cup, stir together cream and flour; whisk cream mixture into broth. Over medium heat, bring to a simmer. Cook about 5 minutes or until sauce thickens, stirring constantly. Return

chicken and vegetables to Dutch oven and simmer 5 to 10 minutes, until heated through. Season to taste with salt, pepper and lemon juice.

Makes 4 servings

Nutty Oven-Fried Chicken Drumsticks

12 chicken drumsticks or 6 legs (about 3 pounds)
1 egg, beaten
1 cup cornflake crumbs
⅓ cup finely chopped pecans
1 tablespoon sugar
1½ teaspoons salt
½ teaspoon onion powder
½ teaspoon black pepper
¼ cup butter or margarine, melted

Preheat oven to 400°F. Toss chicken legs with egg to coat.

Combine cornflakes, pecans, sugar, salt, onion powder and pepper in large resealable plastic food storage bag. Add chicken legs two at a time; shake to coat.

Place chicken on foil-lined baking sheet; drizzle with melted butter. Bake 40 to 45 minutes or until tender.

Makes 4 to 6 servings

Nutty Oven-Fried Chicken Drumsticks

Southern-Style Chicken and Greens

1 teaspoon salt
1 teaspoon paprika
½ teaspoon black pepper
3½ pounds chicken pieces
4 thick slices smoked bacon (4 ounces), cut crosswise into ¼-inch strips
1 cup uncooked rice
1 can (14½ ounces) stewed tomatoes, undrained
1¼ cups chicken broth
2 cups packed coarsely chopped fresh collard or mustard greens or kale (3 to 4 ounces)

Preheat oven to 350°F.

Combine salt, paprika and pepper in small bowl. Sprinkle meaty side of chicken pieces with salt mixture; set aside.

Place bacon in ovenproof Dutch oven; cook over medium heat until crisp. Remove from Dutch oven; drain on paper towels. Reserve drippings.

Heat drippings in Dutch oven over medium-high heat until hot. Arrange chicken in single layer in Dutch oven and cook 3 minutes per side or until chicken is browned. Transfer to plate; set aside. Repeat with remaining pieces. Reserve 1 tablespoon drippings in Dutch oven.

Add rice to drippings; cook and stir 1 minute. Add tomatoes with juice, broth, collard greens and half of bacon; bring to a boil over high heat. Remove from heat; arrange chicken over rice mixture.

Bake, covered, about 40 minutes or until chicken is no longer pink in centers and most of liquid is absorbed. Let stand 5 minutes before serving. Transfer to serving platter; sprinkle with remaining bacon.
Makes 4 to 6 servings

Serving Suggestion: Serve with corn bread or corn muffins.

Swiss 'n' Chicken Casserole

Prep Time: 20 minutes
Cook Time: 40 minutes

4 cups chopped cooked chicken
2 cups KRAFT® Shredded Swiss Cheese
2 cups croutons
2 cups sliced celery
1 cup MIRACLE WHIP® or MIRACLE WHIP® LIGHT Dressing
½ cup milk
¼ cup chopped onion
Chopped walnuts (optional)

• Heat oven to 350°F.

• Mix all ingredients. Spoon into 2-quart casserole. Sprinkle with walnuts, if desired.

• Bake 40 minutes or until thoroughly heated.	*Makes 6 servings*

Southern-Style Chicken and Greens

Bacon & Cheese Stuffed Chicken

Prep Time: 15 minutes
Cook Time: 30 minutes

4 boneless, skinless chicken breast halves (about 1¼ pounds), pounded ¼ inch thick
1 cup shredded mozzarella cheese (about 4 ounces)
4 slices bacon, crisp-cooked and crumbled
1 egg, slightly beaten
½ cup Italian seasoned dry bread crumbs
2 tablespoons olive or vegetable oil
1 jar (26 to 28 ounces) RAGÚ® Hearty Robusto!™ Pasta Sauce
1 cup chicken broth
8 ounces linguine or spaghetti, cooked and drained

1. Evenly top each chicken breast half with cheese and bacon. Roll up and secure with wooden toothpicks. Dip chicken in egg, then bread crumbs.

2. In 12-inch nonstick skillet, heat oil over medium heat and brown chicken, turning occasionally. Stir in Ragú Pasta Sauce and broth. Bring to a boil over high heat. Reduce heat to low and simmer covered 10 minutes or until chicken is no longer pink.

3. To serve, arrange chicken and sauce over hot linguine. Garnish, if desired, with chopped fresh basil or parsley. *Makes 4 servings*

Spicy Fried Chicken

⅓ cup all-purpose flour
2 tablespoons cornmeal
1 teaspoon baking powder
1 package (1.0 ounces) LAWRY'S® Taco Spices & Seasonings
1¼ teaspoons LAWRY'S® Seasoned Salt
1 teaspoon paprika
¾ teaspoon cayenne pepper
½ teaspoon LAWRY'S® Seasoned Pepper
3 to 3½ pounds chicken pieces
¼ cup butter or shortening, melted
2 tablespoons lemon juice

In large resealable plastic food storage bag, combine flour, cornmeal, baking powder, Taco Spices & Seasonings, Seasoned Salt, paprika, cayenne pepper and Seasoned Pepper; mix well. Add chicken, a few pieces at a time, to plastic bag; seal bag. Shake until well coated. Place chicken in shallow baking pan. Combine butter and lemon juice; drizzle over chicken. Bake in 400°F oven 1 hour or until chicken is no longer pink in center.
Makes 6 to 8 servings

Serving Suggestion: Serve with hot buttered corn on the cob and lots of napkins.

Bacon & Cheese Stuffed Chicken

Old-Fashioned Chicken with Dumplings

3 to 3½ pounds chicken pieces
3 tablespoons butter or margarine
2 cans (about 14 ounces each) ready-to-serve chicken broth
3½ cups water
1 teaspoon salt
¼ teaspoon white pepper
2 large carrots, cut into 1-inch slices
2 ribs celery, cut into 1-inch slices
8 to 10 small boiling onions
¼ pound small mushrooms, cut into halves
Parsley Dumplings (recipe follows)
½ cup frozen peas, thawed, drained

Brown chicken in melted butter in 6- to 8-quart saucepan over medium-high heat. Add broth, water, salt and pepper. Bring to a boil over high heat. Reduce heat to low. Cover; simmer 15 minutes. Add carrots, celery, onions and mushrooms. Simmer, covered, 40 minutes or until chicken and vegetables are tender.

Prepare Parsley Dumplings. When chicken is tender, skim fat from broth. Stir in peas. Drop dumpling mixture into broth, making 6 large or 12 small dumplings. Cover; simmer 15 to 20 minutes or until dumplings are firm to the touch and wooden pick inserted in center comes out clean.

Makes 6 servings

Parsley Dumplings: Sift 2 cups all-purpose flour, 4 teaspoons baking powder and ½ teaspoon salt into medium bowl. Cut in 5 tablespoons cold butter until mixture resembles coarse meal. Make a well in center; pour in 1 cup milk, all at once. Add 2 tablespoons chopped parsley; stir with fork until mixture forms a ball.

Garlicky Baked Chicken

1½ cups fresh bread crumbs
3 cloves garlic, minced
1 tablespoon peanut or vegetable oil
2 tablespoons soy sauce
1 tablespoon Chinese hot mustard
1 cut-up whole chicken (about 3½ pounds) *or* 3½ pounds chicken parts, skinned, if desired

1. Preheat oven to 350°F. Combine bread crumbs, garlic and oil in shallow dish.

2. Combine soy sauce and hot mustard in small bowl; brush evenly over chicken. Dip chicken in bread crumb mixture to coat lightly, but evenly. Place on foil-lined baking sheet.

3. Bake chicken 45 to 55 minutes until juices run clear.

Makes 4 to 6 servings

Chicken with Brandied Fruit Sauce

- 4 boneless, skinless chicken breast halves
- ½ teaspoon salt
- ¼ teaspoon ground nutmeg
- 2 tablespoons butter or margarine
- 1 tablespoon cornstarch
- ¼ teaspoon ground red pepper
  Juice of 1 orange
  Juice of 1 lemon
  Juice of 1 lime
- ⅓ cup orange marmalade
- 2 tablespoons brandy
- 1 cup red seedless grapes

Pound chicken to ½-inch thickness on hard surface with meat mallet or rolling pin. Sprinkle salt and nutmeg over chicken. Heat butter in large skillet over medium-high heat. Add chicken and cook, turning, about 8 minutes or until chicken is brown, fork-tender and no longer pink in center. Mix cornstarch and red pepper in small bowl. Stir in orange juice, lemon juice and lime juice; set aside. Remove chicken to serving platter. Add marmalade to same skillet; heat until melted. Stir in juice mixture; cook and stir until mixture boils and thickens. Add brandy and grapes. Return chicken to pan; spoon sauce over chicken. Cook over low heat 5 minutes. *Makes 4 servings*

Favorite recipe from **Delmarva Poultry Industry, Inc.**

Pennsylvania Dutch Chicken Bake

- 1 package (about 1¾ pounds) PERDUE® Fresh Skinless Chicken Thighs
  Salt and pepper to taste
- 1 to 2 tablespoons canola oil
- 1 can (14 to 16 ounces) sauerkraut, undrained
- 1 can (14 to 15 ounces) whole onions, drained
- 1 tart red apple, unpeeled and sliced
- 6 to 8 dried whole apricots
- ½ cup raisins
- ¼ cup brown sugar, or to taste

Preheat oven to 350°F. Season thighs with salt and pepper. In large nonstick skillet over medium-high heat, heat oil. Cook thighs 6 to 8 minutes per side until browned. Meanwhile, in 12×9-inch shallow baking dish, mix sauerkraut, onions, apple, apricots, raisins and brown sugar until blended. Arrange thighs in sauerkraut mixture. Cover and bake 30 to 40 minutes or until chicken is cooked through and a meat thermometer inserted in thickest part of thigh registers 180°F.

Makes 6 servings

Pepper Glazed Cajun Chicken

4 boneless, skinless chicken breast halves
½ to 1 teaspoon Cajun seasoning*
1 tablespoon vegetable oil
¼ cup sliced green onions
6 tablespoons hot pepper jelly
¼ cup defatted chicken broth
2 tablespoons white vinegar

Use larger measurement if hotter flavor is preferred.

Sprinkle Cajun seasoning over chicken. Heat oil in large nonstick skillet over medium-high heat. Add chicken; cook about 10 minutes or until chicken is brown, turning occasionally. Remove chicken and set aside. Add onions to drippings in skillet; cook and stir 2 minutes. Add jelly, broth and vinegar; cook and stir until jelly melts.

Return chicken to pan; spoon glaze over chicken. Cover and cook over medium-low heat about 5 minutes or until chicken is fork-tender and no longer pink in center, turning occasionally.

Remove chicken to serving platter. Increase heat to medium-high and cook until glaze thickens slightly. Spoon glaze over chicken.

Makes 4 servings

Favorite recipe from **Delmarva Poultry Industry, Inc.**

Country Chicken Pot Pie

Prep Time: *5 minutes*
Cook Time: *15 minutes*

1 package (1.8 ounces) white sauce mix
2¼ cups milk
2 to 3 cups diced cooked chicken*
3 cups BIRDS EYE® frozen Mixed Vegetables
1½ cups seasoned croutons**

No leftover cooked chicken handy? Before beginning recipe, cut 1 pound boneless skinless chicken into 1-inch cubes. Brown chicken in 1 tablespoon butter or margarine in large skillet, then proceed with recipe.

**For a quick homemade touch, substitute 4 bakery-bought biscuits for croutons. Split and add to skillet, cut side down.*

• Prepare white sauce mix with milk in large skillet according to package directions.

• Add chicken and vegetables. Bring to boil over medium-high heat; cook 3 minutes or until heated through, stirring occasionally.

• Top with croutons; cover and let stand 5 minutes.

Makes about 4 servings

Serving Suggestion: Serve with a green salad.

Pepper Glazed Cajun Chicken

Hidden Valley Fried Chicken

1 broiler-fryer chicken, cut up
   (2 to 2½ pounds)
1 cup prepared HIDDEN VALLEY®
   Original Ranch® Salad
   Dressing
¾ cup all-purpose flour
1 teaspoon salt
½ teaspoon freshly ground black
   pepper
   Vegetable oil

Place chicken pieces in shallow baking dish; pour salad dressing over chicken. Cover; refrigerate at least 8 hours. Remove chicken. Shake off excess marinade; discard marinade. Preheat oven to 350°F. On plate, mix flour, salt and pepper; roll chicken in seasoned flour. Heat ½ inch oil in large skillet until small cube of bread dropped into oil browns in 60 seconds or until oil is 375°F. Fry chicken until golden, 5 to 7 minutes on each side; transfer to baking pan. Bake until chicken is tender and juices run clear, about 30 minutes. Serve with corn muffins, if desired.

Makes 4 main-dish servings

Hidden Valley Fried Chicken

Classic Chicken Biscuit Pie

12 boneless, skinless chicken tenderloins, cut into 1-inch pieces
4 cups water
2 boxes UNCLE BEN'S® COUNTRY INN®Chicken Flavored Rice
1 can (10¾ ounces) condensed cream of chicken soup
1 bag (1 pound) frozen peas, potatoes and carrots
1 container (12 ounces) refrigerated buttermilk biscuits

1. Heat oven to 400°F. In large saucepan, combine chicken, water, rice, contents of seasoning packets, soup and vegetable mixture; mix well. Bring to a boil. Cover; reduce heat and simmer 10 minutes.

2. Place in 13×9-inch baking pan; top with biscuits.

3. Bake 10 to 12 minutes or until biscuits are golden brown.
Makes 8 to 10 servings

Cook's Tip: For individual pot pies, place rice mixture in small ramekins or casseroles. Proceed with recipe as directed.

Honey Mustard BBQ Chicken Stir-Fry

Prep Time: 10 minutes
Cook Time: 15 minutes

1 box (10 ounces) couscous pasta
1 pound boneless chicken, cut into strips
1 medium red bell pepper, cut into thin strips
1 medium onion, sliced
⅓ cup *French's*® Honey Mustard
⅓ cup barbecue sauce

1. Prepare couscous according to package directions. Keep warm.

2. Heat *1 tablespoon oil* in large nonstick skillet over medium-high heat. Stir-fry chicken in batches 5 to 10 minutes or until browned. Transfer to bowl. Drain fat.

3. Heat *1 tablespoon oil* in same skillet until hot. Stir-fry vegetables 3 minutes or until crisp-tender. Return chicken to skillet. Stir in *⅔ cup water,* mustard and barbecue sauce. Heat to boiling, stirring often. Serve over couscous.
Makes 4 servings

100 BEST
Chicken Recipes

INTERNATIONAL FLAVORS

Asian Chicken and Noodles

Prep Time: *5 minutes*
Cook Time: *20 minutes*

1 package (3 ounces) chicken flavor instant ramen noodles
1 bag (16 ounces) BIRDS EYE® frozen Farm Fresh Mixtures Broccoli, Carrots and Water Chestnuts*
1 tablespoon vegetable oil
1 pound boneless skinless chicken breasts, cut into thin strips
¼ cup stir-fry sauce

*Or, substitute 1 bag (16 ounces) Birds Eye® frozen Broccoli Cuts.

• Reserve seasoning packet from noodles.

• Bring 2 cups water to boil in large saucepan. Add noodles and ' vegetables. Cook 3 minutes, stirring occasionally; drain.

• Meanwhile, heat oil in large nonstick skillet over medium-high heat. Add chicken; cook and stir until browned, about 8 minutes.

• Stir in noodles, vegetables, stir-fry sauce and reserved seasoning packet; heat through.
Makes about 4 servings

Citrus Chicken

1 large orange
1 large lime*
¾ cup WISH-BONE® Italian Dressing
2½ to 3 pounds chicken pieces

Substitution: Omit lime peel. Use 3 tablespoons lime juice.

From the orange, grate enough peel to measure 1½ teaspoons and squeeze enough juice to measure ⅓ cup; set aside.

From the lime, grate enough peel to measure 1 teaspoon and squeeze enough juice to measure 3 tablespoons; set aside.

For marinade, combine Italian dressing, orange and lime juices and orange and lime peels. In large, shallow nonaluminum baking dish or plastic bag, pour ¾ cup marinade over chicken; turn to coat. Cover, or close bag, and marinate in refrigerator, turning occasionally, 3 to 24 hours. Refrigerate remaining ½ cup marinade.

Remove chicken from marinade, discarding marinade. Grill or broil chicken, turning once and brushing frequently with refrigerated marinade, until chicken is no longer pink.
Makes 4 servings

Variation: Also terrific with WISH-BONE® Robusto Italian or Just 2 Good Italian Dressing.

Chicken Vesuvio

1 whole chicken
(about 3¾ pounds)
¼ cup olive oil
3 tablespoons lemon juice
4 cloves garlic, minced
3 large baking potatoes
Salt and lemon pepper

Preheat oven to 375°F. Place chicken, breast side down, on rack in large shallow roasting pan. Combine olive oil, lemon juice and garlic; brush half of oil mixture over chicken. Set aside remaining oil mixture. Roast chicken, uncovered, 30 minutes.

Meanwhile, peel potatoes; cut lengthwise into quarters. Turn chicken, breast side up. Arrange potatoes around chicken in roasting pan. Brush chicken and potatoes with remaining oil mixture; sprinkle with salt and lemon pepper seasoning to taste. Roast chicken and potatoes, basting occasionally with pan juices, 50 minutes or until meat thermometer inserted into thickest part of chicken thigh, not touching bone, registers 180°F and potatoes are tender.
Makes 4 to 6 servings

Chicken Vesuvio

Jerk Chicken and Pasta

Jerk Sauce (recipe follows)
12 ounces boneless skinless chicken breasts
Nonstick cooking spray
1 cup canned fat-free reduced-sodium chicken broth
1 green bell pepper, sliced
2 green onions with tops, sliced
8 ounces uncooked fettuccine, cooked and kept warm
Grated Parmesan cheese (optional)

1. Spread Jerk Sauce on both sides of chicken. Place in glass dish; refrigerate, covered, 15 to 30 minutes.

2. Spray medium skillet with cooking spray. Heat over medium heat until hot. Add chicken; cook 5 to 10 minutes or until browned and no longer pink in center. Add chicken broth, bell pepper and onions; bring to a boil. Reduce heat and simmer, uncovered, 5 to 7 minutes or until vegetables are crisp-tender and broth is reduced to thin sauce consistency.

3. Remove chicken from skillet and cut into slices. Toss fettuccine, chicken and vegetable mixture in large serving bowl. Sprinkle with Parmesan cheese, if desired.

Makes 4 main-dish servings

Jerk Sauce

¼ cup loosely packed fresh cilantro
2 tablespoons coarsely chopped fresh ginger
2 tablespoons black pepper
2 tablespoons lime juice
3 cloves garlic
1 tablespoon ground allspice
½ teaspoon curry powder
¼ teaspoon ground cloves
⅛ teaspoon ground red pepper

Combine all ingredients in food processor or blender; process until thick paste consistency.

Makes about ¼ cup

Grilled Italian Chicken

½ cup prepared HIDDEN VALLEY® Ranch Italian Salad Dressing
1 tablespoon Dijon-style mustard
4 boned chicken breast halves

In small bowl or measuring cup, whisk together salad dressing and mustard; reserve 3 tablespoons for final baste. Brush chicken generously with some of remaining dressing mixture. Grill or broil, basting several times with dressing mixture, until chicken is golden and cooked through, about 5 minutes on each side. Brush generously with reserved dressing just before removing from grill.

Makes 4 servings

Jerk Chicken and Pasta

Classic Chicken Parmesan

6 boneless, skinless chicken breast halves, pounded thin (about 1½ pounds)
2 eggs, slightly beaten
1 cup Italian seasoned dry bread crumbs
2 tablespoons olive or vegetable oil
1 jar (26 to 28 ounces) RAGÚ® Old World Style® Pasta Sauce
1 cup shredded mozzarella cheese (about 4 ounces)

Preheat oven to 375°F. Dip chicken in eggs, then bread crumbs, coating well.

In 12-inch skillet, heat oil over medium-high heat and brown chicken; drain on paper towels.

In 11×7-inch baking dish, evenly spread 1 cup Ragú® Old World Style Pasta Sauce. Arrange chicken in dish, then top with remaining sauce. Sprinkle with mozzarella cheese and, if desired, grated Parmesan cheese. Bake 25 minutes or until chicken is no longer pink.   *Makes 6 servings*

Recipe Tip: To pound chicken, place a boneless, skinless breast between two sheets of waxed paper. Use a rolling pin to press down and out from the center to flatten.

Kung Pao Chicken

1 pound boneless, skinless chicken breasts, cut into 1-inch pieces
1 tablespoon cornstarch
2 teaspoons CRISCO® Oil*
3 tablespoons chopped green onions with tops
2 cloves garlic, minced
¼ to 1½ teaspoons crushed red pepper
¼ to ½ teaspoon ground ginger
¼ cup rice vinegar
¼ cup soy sauce
1 tablespoon sugar
⅓ cup unsalted dry roasted peanuts
4 cups hot cooked rice (cooked without salt or fat)

*Use your favorite Crisco Oil product.

1. Combine chicken and cornstarch in small bowl; toss. Heat oil in large skillet or wok on medium-high heat. Add chicken. Stir-fry 5 to 7 minutes or until no longer pink in center. Remove from skillet. Add onions, garlic, red pepper and ginger to skillet. Stir-fry 15 seconds. Remove from heat.

2. Combine vinegar, soy sauce and sugar in small bowl. Stir well. Add to skillet. Return chicken to skillet. Stir until coated. Stir in nuts. Heat thoroughly, stirring occasionally. Serve over hot rice.   *Makes 4 servings*

Chicken Burritos

1 package (8) ORTEGA® Burrito
   Dinner Kit (flour tortillas and
   burrito seasoning mix)
1 tablespoon vegetable oil
1 pound (3 to 4) boneless,
   skinless chicken breast
   halves, cut into 2-inch strips
1½ cups water
   Toppings: shredded Cheddar
   cheese, shredded iceberg
   lettuce, chopped green
   onions, sliced ripe olives and
   ORTEGA® Thick & Chunky
   Salsa, hot, medium or mild

HEAT oil in large skillet over medium-high heat. Add chicken. Cook for 3 to 4 minutes or until no longer pink in center. Add burrito seasoning mix and water. Bring to a boil. Reduce heat to low; cook, stirring occasionally, for 5 to 6 minutes or until mixture is thickened.

REMOVE tortillas from outer plastic pouch. Microwave on HIGH (100%) power for 10 to 15 seconds or until warm. Or heat each tortilla, turning frequently, in small skillet over medium-high heat until warm.

SPREAD chicken mixture over tortillas. Top with cheese, lettuce, green onions, olives and salsa. Fold into burritos.   *Makes 8 burritos*

Polynesian Chicken and Rice

Prep Time: 20 minutes
Cook Time: 10 minutes

1 can (20 ounces) DOLE®
   Pineapple Tidbits or
   Pineapple Chunks
½ cup DOLE® Seedless or Golden
   Raisins
½ cup sliced green onions
2 teaspoons finely chopped fresh
   ginger *or* ½ teaspoon ground
   ginger
1 clove garlic, finely chopped
3 cups cooked white or brown
   rice
2 cups chopped cooked chicken
   breast or turkey breast
2 tablespoons low-sodium soy
   sauce

• Drain pineapple; reserve 4 tablespoons juice.

• Heat 2 tablespoons reserved juice over medium heat in large, nonstick skillet. Add raisins, green onions, ginger and garlic; cook and stir 3 minutes.

• Stir in pineapple, rice, chicken, soy sauce and remaining 2 tablespoons juice. Cover; reduce heat to low and cook 5 minutes more or until heated through. Garnish with cherry tomatoes and green onions, if desired.
                    Makes 4 servings

Chicken Marsala

6 ounces uncooked broad egg noodles
½ cup Italian-style bread crumbs
1 teaspoon dried basil leaves
1 egg
1 teaspoon water
4 boneless skinless chicken breast halves
3 tablespoons olive oil, divided
¾ cup chopped onion
8 ounces button mushrooms, sliced
3 cloves garlic, minced
3 tablespoons all-purpose flour
1 can (14½ ounces) chicken broth
½ cup dry marsala wine
¾ teaspoon salt
¾ teaspoon black pepper
Chopped fresh parsley

Preheat oven to 375°F. Spray 11X7-inch baking dish with nonstick cooking spray. Cook Noodles according to package directions; drain and place in prepared dish.

Meanwhile, combine bread crumbs and basil on shallow plate. Beat egg with water in medium bowl. Dip chicken in egg mixture; then roll in crumb mixture, patting to coat. Heat 2 tablespoons oil in large skillet over medium heat until hot. Cook chicken 3 minutes per side or until browned; set aside.

Heat remaining 1 tablespoon oil in same skillet over medium heat. Add onion; cook and stir 5 minutes. Add mushrooms and garlic; cook and stir 3 minutes. Sprinkle flour over onion mixture; cook and stir 1 minute. Add broth, wine, salt and pepper; bring to boil over high heat. Cook and stir 5 minutes or until sauce thickens. Reserve ½ cup sauce. Pour remaining sauce over noodles; stir until noodles are well coated. Place chicken on top of noodles. Spoon reserved sauce over chicken.

Bake uncovered, 20 minutes or until chicken is no longer pink in center. Sprinkle with parsley.

Makes 4 servings

Simple Stir-Fry

1 tablespoon vegetable oil
12 boneless, skinless chicken tenderloins, cut into 1-inch pieces
1 bag (1 pound) frozen stir-fry vegetable mix
2 tablespoons soy sauce
2 tablespoons honey
2 (2-cup) bags UNCLE BEN'S® Boil-in-Bag Rice

1. Heat oil in large skillet or wok. Add chicken; cook over medium-high heat 6 to 8 minutes or until lightly browned. Add vegetables, soy sauce and honey. Cover and cook 5 to 8 minutes or until chicken is no longer pink in center and vegetables are crisp-tender.

2. Meanwhile, cook rice according to package directions. Serve stir-fry over rice. *Makes 4 servings*

Simple Stir-Fry

Soy Honey Chicken

½ **cup honey**
½ **cup soy sauce**
¼ **cup dry sherry or water**
1 **teaspoon grated fresh gingerroot***
2 **medium cloves garlic, crushed**
1 **broiler-fryer chicken, cut into serving pieces (2½ to 3 pounds)**

Substitute 2 teaspoons ground ginger for fresh gingerroot, if desired.

Combine honey, soy sauce, sherry, gingerroot and garlic in small bowl. Place chicken in plastic food storage bag or large glass baking dish. Pour honey marinade over chicken, turning chicken to coat. Close bag or cover dish with plastic wrap. Marinate in refrigerator at least 6 hours, turning two or three times.

Remove chicken from marinade; reserve marinade. Arrange chicken on rack over roasting pan. Cover chicken with foil. Bake at 350°F 30 minutes. Bring reserved marinade to a boil in small saucepan over medium heat; boil 3 minutes and set aside.

Uncover chicken; brush with marinade. Bake, uncovered, 30 to 45 minutes longer or until juices run clear and chicken is no longer pink, brushing occasionally with marinade.

Makes 4 servings

Favorite recipe from **National Honey Board**

Spanish Skillet Supper

Prep Time: *5 minutes*
Cook Time: *20 minutes*

1 **tablespoon vegetable oil**
1 **pound boneless skinless chicken breasts, cut into 1-inch cubes**
2 **cups hot water**
1 **package (4.4 ounces) Spanish rice and sauce mix**
2 **cups BIRDS EYE® frozen Green Peas**
Crushed red pepper flakes

• Heat oil in large skillet over medium-high heat. Add chicken; cook and stir until lightly browned, about 5 minutes.

• Add hot water, rice and sauce mix; bring to boil. Reduce heat to medium-low; simmer, uncovered, 5 minutes.

• Stir in green peas; increase heat to medium-high. Cover and cook 5 minutes or until peas and rice are tender.

• Sprinkle with red pepper flakes.
Makes about 4 servings

Grilled Chicken with Asian Pesto

**4 boneless skinless chicken
  breast halves *or* 8 boneless
  skinless thighs *or* combination
  of both
Olive or vegetable oil
Salt and black pepper
Asian Pesto (recipe follows)
Lime wedges**

Place chicken between two pieces of waxed paper; pound to ⅜-inch thickness. Brush chicken with oil; season to taste with salt and pepper. Spread about ½ tablespoon Asian Pesto on both sides of each breast or thigh.

Oil hot grid to help prevent sticking. Grill chicken, on an uncovered grill, over medium KINGSFORD® Briquets, 6 to 8 minutes until chicken is cooked through, turning once. Serve with additional Asian Pesto and lime wedges.   *Makes 4 servings*

Asian Pesto

**1 cup packed fresh basil
1 cup packed fresh cilantro
1 cup packed fresh mint leaves
¼ cup olive or vegetable oil
2 cloves garlic, chopped
2½ to 3½ tablespoons lime juice
1 tablespoon sugar
1 teaspoon salt
1 teaspoon black pepper**

Combine all ingredients in a blender or food processor; process until smooth.   *Makes about ¾ cup*

Note: The Asian Pesto recipe makes enough for 6 servings. Leftovers can be saved and used as a spread for sandwiches.

Chicken with Roasted Garlic Marinara

Prep: 10 minutes
Cook: 5 minutes

**1 package (9 ounces)
  DI GIORNO® Angel's Hair
1 package (6 ounces) LOUIS
  RICH® Italian Style or Grilled
  Chicken Breast Strips
1 package (10 ounces)
  DI GIORNO® Roasted Garlic
  Marinara Sauce
DI GIORNO® Shredded
  Parmesan Cheese**

PREPARE pasta as directed on package; drain.

MIX chicken breast strips and sauce in saucepan. Cook on medium heat 5 minutes or until thoroughly heated.

SERVE over pasta; sprinkle with cheese.   *Makes 3 to 4 servings*

Jamaican Grilled Chicken

Prep Time: 15 minutes
Marinate Time: 1 hour
Cook Time: 45 minutes

1 whole chicken (4 pounds), cut into pieces *or* 6 whole chicken legs
1 cup coarsely chopped fresh cilantro leaves and stems
½ cup *Frank's® RedHot®* Sauce
⅓ cup vegetable oil
6 cloves garlic, coarsely chopped
¼ cup fresh lime juice (juice of 2 limes)
1 teaspoon grated lime peel
1 teaspoon ground turmeric
1 teaspoon ground allspice

1. Loosen and pull back skin from chicken pieces. Do not remove skin. Place chicken pieces in large resealable plastic food storage bag or large glass bowl.

2. Place remaining ingredients in blender or food processor. Cover; process until smooth. Reserve ⅓ cup marinade. Pour remaining marinade over chicken pieces, turning to coat evenly. Seal bags or cover bowl; refrigerate 1 hour.

3. Prepare grill. Reposition skin on chicken pieces. Place chicken on oiled grid. Grill, over medium to medium-low coals, 45 minutes or until chicken is no longer pink near bone and juices run clear, turning and basting often with reserved marinade.
Makes 6 servings

Chicken di Napolitano

1 tablespoon olive oil
2 boneless, skinless chicken breasts (about 8 ounces)
1 can (14½ ounces) diced tomatoes, undrained
1¼ cups water
1 box UNCLE BEN'S® Rice Pilaf
¼ cup chopped fresh basil *or* 1½ teaspoons dried basil leaves

1. Heat oil in large skillet. Add chicken, cook over medium-high heat 8 to 10 minutes or until lightly browned on both sides.

2. Add tomatoes, water, rice and contents of seasoning packet. Bring to a boil. Cover; reduce heat and simmer 15 to 18 minutes or until chicken is no longer pink in center and liquid is absorbed.

3. Stir in basil. Slice chicken and serve over rice. *Makes 2 servings*

Cook's Tip: For more flavor, substitute diced tomatoes with Italian herbs or roasted garlic for diced tomatoes.

Jamaican Grilled Chicken

Chicken Walnut Stir-Fry

Sauce
- ⅔ **cup chicken broth**
- 1½ **tablespoons LA CHOY® Soy Sauce**
- 1 **tablespoon** *each:* **cornstarch and dry sherry**
- ½ **teaspoon sugar**
- ¼ **teaspoon** *each:* **pepper and Oriental sesame oil**

Chicken and Vegetables
- 2 **tablespoons cornstarch**
- 2 **teaspoons LA CHOY® Soy Sauce**
- 2 **teaspoons dry sherry**
- 1 **pound boneless skinless chicken breasts, cut into thin 2-inch strips**
- 4 **tablespoons WESSON® Oil, divided**
- 2½ **cups fresh broccoli flowerettes**
- 1½ **teaspoons minced fresh garlic**
- 1 **teaspoon minced ginger root**
- 1 **(8-ounce) can LA CHOY® Bamboo Shoots, drained**
- 1 **cup toasted chopped walnuts**
- 1 **(6-ounce) package frozen pea pods, thawed and drained**
- 1 **(5-ounce) can LA CHOY® Chow Mein Noodles**

In small bowl, combine sauce ingredients; set aside. In separate small bowl, combine cornstarch, soy sauce and sherry; mix well. Add chicken; toss gently to coat. In large nonstick skillet or wok, heat 3 tablespoons Wesson Oil. Add half of chicken mixture; stir-fry until chicken is no longer pink in center. Remove chicken from skillet; set aside. Repeat with remaining chicken mixture. Heat remaining 1 tablespoon Wesson Oil in same skillet. Add broccoli, garlic and ginger; stir-fry until broccoli is crisp-tender. Return chicken mixture to skillet with bamboo shoots, walnuts and pea pods; heat thoroughly, stirring occasionally. Stir sauce; add to skillet. Cook, stirring constantly, until sauce is thick and bubbly. Garnish with La Choy Chow Mein Noodles, if desired.   *Makes 4 to 6 servings*

Mandarin Orange Chicken

- ½ **(6-ounce) can frozen orange juice concentrate, thawed**
- ⅓ **cup HOLLAND HOUSE® White Cooking Wine**
- ¼ **cup orange marmalade**
- ½ **teaspoon ground ginger**
- 4 **boneless chicken breast halves, skinned (about 1 pound)**
- 1 **(11-ounce) can mandarin orange segments, drained**
- ½ **cup green grapes, halved**

Heat oven to 350°F. In 12×8-inch (2-quart) baking dish, combine concentrate, cooking wine, marmalade and ginger; mix well. Add chicken; turn to coat. Bake at 350°F for 45 to 60 minutes, or until chicken is tender and no longer pink, basting occasionally and adding orange segments and grapes during last 5 minutes of cooking.

Makes 4 servings

Chicken Walnut Stir-Fry

Spicy Mango Chicken

¼ cup mango nectar
¼ cup chopped fresh cilantro
2 jalapeño chile peppers,
   seeded and finely chopped
2 teaspoons vegetable oil
2 teaspoons LAWRY'S® Seasoned
   Salt
½ teaspoon LAWRY'S® Garlic
   Powder with Parsley
½ teaspoon ground cumin
4 boneless, skinless chicken
   breast halves (about
   1 pound)
   Mango & Black Bean Salsa
   (recipe follows)

In small bowl, combine all ingredients
except chicken and salsa; mix well.
Brush marinade on both sides of
chicken. Grill or broil chicken 10 to
15 minutes or until no longer pink in
center and juices run clear when cut,
turning once and basting often with
additional marinade. *Do not baste
during last 5 minutes of cooking.*
Discard any remaining marinade. Top
chicken with Mango & Black Bean
Salsa.   *Makes 4 servings*

Hint: Jalapeño peppers can sting and
irritate the skin; wear rubber gloves
when handling peppers and do not
touch eyes.

Mango & Black Bean Salsa

1 ripe mango, peeled, seeded
   and chopped
1 cup canned black beans,
   rinsed and drained
½ cup chopped tomato
2 thinly sliced green onions
1 tablespoon chopped fresh
   cilantro
1½ teaspoons lime juice
1½ teaspoons red wine vinegar
½ teaspoon LAWRY'S® Seasoned
   Salt

In medium bowl, combine all
ingredients; mix well. Let stand
30 minutes to allow flavors to blend.
                Makes about 2¾ cups

Serving Suggestion: Serve with
chicken or fish.

Spicy Mango Chicken

1OO BEST
Chicken Recipes

HOT OFF THE GRILL

Hot 'n' Spicy Chicken Barbecue

- **½ cup A.1.® Steak Sauce**
- **½ cup tomato sauce**
- **¼ cup finely chopped onion**
- **2 tablespoons cider vinegar**
- **2 tablespoons maple syrup**
- **1 tablespoon vegetable oil**
- **2 teaspoons chili powder**
- **½ teaspoon crushed red pepper flakes**
- **1 (3-pound) chicken, cut up**

Blend steak sauce, tomato sauce, onion, vinegar, maple syrup, oil, chili powder and red pepper flakes in medium saucepan. Heat mixture to a boil over medium heat; reduce heat. Simmer for 5 to 7 minutes or until thickened; cool.

Grill chicken over medium heat for 30 to 40 minutes or until done, turning and basting frequently with prepared sauce. Serve hot.

Makes 4 servings

Grilled Chicken and Apple with Fresh Rosemary

½ cup apple juice
¼ cup white wine vinegar
¼ cup vegetable oil or light olive oil
1 tablespoon chopped fresh rosemary *or* 1 teaspoon dried rosemary leaves, crushed
¼ teaspoon salt
¼ teaspoon ground black pepper
3 boneless skinless chicken breasts, halved
2 Washington Golden Delicious apples, cored and sliced into ½-inch-thick rings

1. Combine juice, vinegar, oil, rosemary, salt and pepper in shallow baking dish or bowl. Add chicken and apples; marinate in refrigerator at least 30 minutes.

2. Heat grill. Remove chicken and apples from marinade; arrange on hot grill. Discard marinade. Cook chicken 20 minutes or until cooked through, turning to grill both sides. Cook and turn apples about 6 minutes or until crisp-tender. Serve.

Makes 6 servings

Favorite recipe from **Washington Apple Commission**

Lime-Mustard Marinated Chicken

2 boneless skinless chicken breast halves (about 3 ounces each)
¼ cup fresh lime juice
3 tablespoons honey mustard, divided
2 teaspoons olive oil
¼ teaspoon ground cumin
⅛ teaspoon ground red pepper
¾ cup plus 2 tablespoons chicken broth, divided
¼ cup uncooked rice
1 cup broccoli florets
⅓ cup matchstick carrots

1. Place chicken in resealable plastic food storage bag. Whisk together lime juice, 2 tablespoons mustard, olive oil, cumin and red pepper. Pour over chicken. Seal bag. Marinate in refrigerator 2 hours.

2. Combine ¾ cup chicken broth, rice and remaining 1 tablespoon mustard in small saucepan. Bring to a boil. Reduce heat and simmer, covered, 12 minutes or until rice is almost tender. Stir in broccoli, carrots, and remaining 2 tablespoons chicken broth. Cook, covered, 2 to 3 minutes more or until vegetables are crisp-tender and rice is tender.

3. Drain chicken; discard marinade. Prepare grill for direct grilling. Grill chicken over medium coals 10 to 13 minutes or until no longer pink in center. Serve chicken with rice mixture. *Makes 2 servings*

Peppery Grilled Salad

1 package (about 1½ pounds) PERDUE® FIT 'N EASY® Fresh Skinless & Boneless Chicken Thighs
1 teaspoon coarsely ground or cracked pepper
3 tablespoons Worcestershire sauce, divided
6 tablespoons olive oil, divided Salt
1 tablespoon Dijon mustard
2 tablespoons wine vinegar
1 tablespoon minced shallots
1 small head bibb or Boston lettuce, torn into pieces
1 bunch arugula, well rinsed, torn into pieces
1 head Belgian endive, torn into pieces
½ pound green beans, cooked tender-crisp
1 cup cherry tomatoes
1 tablespoon minced fresh basil
1 tablespoon minced parsley

Open thighs and pound to flatten to even thickness. Press pepper into both sides of chicken and place in a shallow baking dish. Add 2 tablespoons Worcestershire sauce; turn chicken to coat well. Cover and refrigerate 1 hour or longer.

Prepare grill for cooking. Brush chicken with 1 tablespoon oil and sprinkle lightly with salt. Grill thighs, uncovered, 5 to 6 inches over medium-hot coals 25 to 30 minutes or until chicken is cooked through, turning occasionally.

In salad bowl, combine remaining Worcestershire, mustard, vinegar and shallots. Gradually whisk in remaining oil. Slice warm thighs and add any meat juices to dressing. Arrange greens around edges of 4 dinner plates. Toss chicken, beans and tomatoes with dressing and mound equal portions in middle of greens. To serve, drizzle salads with any remaining dressing and sprinkle with minced herbs. *Makes 4 servings*

Chicken and Fruit Kabobs

1¾ cups honey
¾ cup fresh lemon juice
½ cup Dijon-style mustard
⅓ cup chopped fresh ginger
4 pounds boneless skinless chicken breasts, cut up
6 fresh plums, pitted and quartered
3 firm bananas, cut into chunks
4 cups fresh pineapple chunks (about half of medium pineapple)

Combine honey, lemon juice, mustard and ginger in small bowl; mix well. Thread chicken and fruit onto skewers, alternating chicken with fruit; brush generously with honey mixture. Place kabobs on grill about 4 inches from heat. Grill 5 minutes on each side, brushing frequently with honey mixture. Grill 10 minutes or until chicken is no longer pink in center, turning and brushing frequently with remaining honey mixture.
Makes 12 servings

81

Southwest Chicken

2 tablespoons olive oil
1 clove garlic, pressed
1 teaspoon chili powder
1 teaspoon ground cumin
1 teaspoon dried oregano leaves
½ teaspoon salt
1 pound skinless boneless chicken breast halves or thighs

Combine oil, garlic, chili powder, cumin, oregano and salt; brush over both sides of chicken to coat. Grill chicken over medium-hot KINGSFORD® Briquets 8 to 10 minutes or until chicken is no longer pink, turning once. Serve immediately or use in Build a Burrito, Taco Salad or other favorite recipes.

Makes 4 servings

Note: Southwest Chicken can be grilled ahead and refrigerated for several days or frozen for longer storage.

Build a Burrito: Top warm large flour tortillas with strips of Southwest Chicken and your choice of drained canned black beans, cooked brown or white rice, shredded cheese, salsa verde, shredded lettuce, sliced black olives and chopped cilantro. Fold in sides and roll to enclose filling. Heat in microwave oven at HIGH until heated through. (Or, wrap in foil and heat in preheated 350°F oven.)

Taco Salad: For a quick one-dish meal, layer strips of Southwest Chicken with tomato wedges, blue or traditional corn tortilla chips, sliced black olives, shredded romaine or iceberg lettuce, shredded cheese and avocado slices. Serve with salsa, sour cream, guacamole or a favorite dressing.

Grilled Greek Chicken

1 cup MIRACLE WHIP® Salad Dressing
½ cup chopped fresh parsley
¼ cup dry white wine or chicken broth
1 lemon, sliced and halved
2 tablespoons dried oregano leaves, crushed
1 tablespoon garlic powder
1 tablespoon black pepper
2 (2½- to 3-pound) broiler-fryers, cut up

• Mix together all ingredients except chicken until well blended. Pour over chicken. Cover; marinate in refrigerator at least 20 minutes. Drain marinade; discard.

• Place chicken on grill over medium-hot coals (coals will have slight glow). Grill, covered, 20 to 25 minutes on each side or until tender.

Makes 8 servings

Southwest Chicken

Chicken Shish-Kebabs

¼ cup CRISCO® Oil*
¼ cup wine vinegar
¼ cup lemon juice
1 teaspoon dried oregano leaves
1 clove garlic, minced
¼ teaspoon black pepper
1½ pounds boneless, skinless chicken breasts, cut into 1- to 1½-inch cubes
12 bamboo or metal skewers (10 to 12 inches long)
2 medium tomatoes, cut into wedges
2 medium onions, cut into wedges
1 medium green bell pepper, cut into 1-inch squares
1 medium red bell pepper, cut into 1-inch squares
4 cups hot cooked brown rice (cooked without salt or fat)
Salt (optional)

*Use your favorite Crisco Oil product.

1. Combine oil, vinegar, lemon juice, oregano, garlic and black pepper in shallow baking dish or glass bowl. Stir well. Add chicken. Stir to coat. Cover. Marinate in refrigerator 3 hours, turning chicken several times.

2. Soak bamboo skewers in water. Heat broiler or prepare grill. Thread chicken, tomatoes, onions and bell peppers alternately on skewers.

3. Place skewers on broiler pan or grill. Broil or grill 5 minutes. Turn. Broil or grill 5 to 7 minutes or to desired doneness. Serve over hot rice. Season with salt and garnish, if desired.

Makes 6 servings

Crunchy Apple Salsa with Grilled Chicken

2 cups Washington Gala apples, halved, cored and chopped
¾ cup (1 large) Anaheim chili pepper, seeded and chopped
½ cup chopped onion
¼ cup lime juice
Salt and black pepper to taste
Grilled Chicken (recipe follows)

Combine all ingredients except chicken and mix well; set aside to allow flavors to blend about 45 minutes. Prepare Grilled Chicken. Serve salsa over or alongside Grilled Chicken. *Makes 3 cups salsa*

Grilled Chicken: Marinate 2 whole boneless, skinless chicken breasts in a mixture of ¼ cup dry white wine, ¼ cup apple juice, ½ teaspoon grated lime peel, ½ teaspoon salt and dash pepper for 20 to 30 minutes. Drain and grill over medium-hot coals, turning once, until chicken is no longer pink in center.

Favorite recipe from **Washington Apple Commission**

Crunchy Apple Salsa with Grilled Chicken

Family Barbecued Chicken

5 pounds chicken pieces
1 cup salad oil
⅓ cup tarragon vinegar
¼ cup sugar
¼ cup ketchup
1 tablespoon Worcestershire sauce
1½ teaspoons dry mustard
1 teaspoon LAWRY'S® Red Pepper Seasoned Salt
1 teaspoon LAWRY'S® Garlic Powder with Parsley

In large resealable plastic food storage bag, combine all ingredients except chicken; mix well. Remove ½ cup marinade for basting. Add chicken; seal bag. Marinate in refrigerator at least 30 minutes. Remove chicken; discard used marinade. To partially cook chicken, place in 13×9-inch baking dish. Bake in 350°F oven 45 minutes. Then, grill or broil chicken 15 to 25 minutes depending on size of piece, turning once and basting often with additional ½ cup marinade. Chicken is done when no longer pink in center and juices run clear when cut. *Do not baste during last 5 minutes of cooking.* Discard any remaining marinade.
Makes 6 servings

Serving Suggestion: Serve with baked beans and a fresh vegetable salad.

Santa Fe Grilled Chicken

Juice of 2 to 3 fresh limes (½ cup), divided
2 tablespoons vegetable oil, divided
1 package (about 3 pounds) PERDUE® Fresh Skinless Pick of the Chicken
Salt and black pepper to taste
1 cup fresh or frozen diced peaches
¼ cup finely chopped red onion
1 jalapeño pepper, seeded and minced
2 cloves garlic, minced
1 teaspoon ground cumin
Chili powder

In medium-sized bowl, combine 7 tablespoons lime juice and 1 tablespoon plus 1½ teaspoons oil. Add chicken, salt and pepper; cover and marinate in the refrigerator 2 to 4 hours. Meanwhile to prepare salsa, in small bowl, combine remaining 1 tablespoon lime juice and 1½ teaspoons oil, peaches, onion, jalapeño pepper, garlic and cumin.

Prepare outdoor grill or preheat broiler. Remove chicken from marinade. Sprinkle with chili powder and place on cooking surface of grill over medium-hot coals or on broiler pan. Grill or broil 6 to 8 inches from heat source, allowing 20 to 30 minutes for breasts and 30 to 40 minutes for thighs and drumsticks, turning occasionally. Serve grilled chicken with salsa. *Makes 4 to 5 servings*

Classic Grilled Chicken

1 whole frying chicken*
  (3½ pounds), quartered
¼ cup lemon juice
¼ cup olive oil
2 tablespoons soy sauce
2 large cloves garlic, minced
½ teaspoon sugar
½ teaspoon ground cumin
¼ teaspoon black pepper

*Substitute 3½ pounds chicken parts for whole chicken, if desired. Grill legs and thighs about 35 minutes and breast halves about 25 minutes or until chicken is no longer pink in center, turning once.

Rinse chicken under cold running water; pat dry with paper towels.

Arrange chicken in 13×9×2-inch glass baking dish. Combine remaining ingredients in small bowl; pour half of mixture over chicken. Cover and refrigerate chicken at least 1 hour or overnight. Cover and reserve remaining mixture in refrigerator to use for basting. Remove chicken from marinade; discard marinade. Arrange medium KINGSFORD® Briquets on each side of large rectangular metal or foil drip pan. Pour hot tap water into drip pan until half full. Place chicken on grid directly above drip pan. Grill chicken, skin side down, on covered grill 25 minutes. Baste with reserved baste. Turn chicken; cook 20 to 25 minutes or until juices run clear and chicken is no longer pink in center. *Makes 6 servings*

Classic Grilled Chicken

Grilled Chicken and Vegetable Kabobs

⅓ cup olive oil
¼ cup lemon juice
4 cloves garlic, coarsely chopped
½ teaspoon salt
½ teaspoon lemon pepper
½ teaspoon dried tarragon leaves
1 pound chicken tenders
6 ounces mushrooms
1 cup sliced zucchini
½ cup cubed green bell pepper
½ cup cubed red bell pepper
1 red onion, quartered
6 cherry tomatoes
3 cups hot cooked rice

Combine oil, lemon juice, garlic, salt, lemon pepper and tarragon in large resealable plastic food storage bag. Add chicken, mushrooms, zucchini, bell peppers, onion and tomatoes. Seal and shake until well coated. Refrigerate at least 8 hours, turning occasionally.

Soak 6 (10-inch) wooden skewers in water 30 minutes; set aside.

Remove chicken and vegetables from marinade; discard marinade. Thread chicken and vegetables onto skewers.

Coat grill grid with nonstick cooking spray; place skewers on grid. Grill covered over medium-hot coals 3 to 4 minutes on each side or until chicken is no longer pink in center.

Remove chicken and vegetables from skewers and serve over rice.

Makes 6 servings

Serving Suggestion: Serve with sliced fresh pineapple and green grapes.

Grilled Vegetable and Chicken Pasta

Prep and Cook Time: 16 minutes

8 ounces (4 cups) uncooked bow-tie pasta
2 red or green bell peppers, seeded and cut into quarters
1 medium zucchini, cut into halves
3 boneless skinless chicken breast halves (about 1 pound)
½ cup Italian dressing
½ cup prepared pesto sauce

1. Cook pasta according to package directions. Drain; place in large bowl. Cover to keep warm.

2. While pasta is cooking, combine vegetables, chicken and dressing in medium bowl; toss well. Grill or broil 6 to 8 minutes on each side or until vegetables are crisp-tender and chicken is no longer pink in center. (Vegetables may take less time than chicken.)

3. Cut vegetables and chicken into bite-sized pieces. Add vegetables, chicken and pesto to pasta; toss well.

Makes 4 to 6 servings

Grilled Chicken and Vegetable Kabobs

Grilled Chicken Croissant with Roasted Pepper Dressing

Prep Time: *15 minutes*
Cook Time: *15 minutes*

- ½ **cup** *French's*® **Dijon Mustard**
- 3 **tablespoons olive oil**
- 3 **tablespoons red wine vinegar**
- ¾ **teaspoon dried Italian seasoning**
- ¾ **teaspoon garlic powder**
- 1 **jar (7 ounces) roasted red peppers, drained**
- 1 **pound boneless skinless chicken breast halves**
  Lettuce leaves
- 4 **croissants, split**

Whisk together mustard, oil, vinegar, Italian seasoning and garlic in small bowl until well blended. Pour ¼ cup mixture into blender. Add peppers. Cover and process until mixture is smooth; set aside.

Brush chicken pieces with remaining mustard mixture. Place pieces on grid. Grill over hot coals 15 minutes or until chicken is no longer pink in center, turning often. To serve, place lettuce leaves on bottom halves of croissants. Arrange chicken on top of lettuce. Spoon roasted pepper dressing over chicken. Cover with croissant top. Garnish as desired.

Makes 4 servings

San Francisco Grilled Chicken

- 2 **boneless, skinless chicken breast halves**
- 3 **tablespoons Italian or Ranch salad dressing**
- 2 **slices SARGENTO® Deli Style Sliced Muenster or Swiss Cheese**
- 2 **kaiser rolls, split** *or* **4 slices sourdough bread**
- 8 **spinach leaves**
- ½ **cup alfalfa sprouts**
- 6 **avocado slices**
- 2 **tablespoons thick salsa**

Pound chicken breast halves to ¼-inch thickness. Place in shallow bowl; pour dressing over chicken. Cover; marinate in refrigerator 1 hour. Drain chicken. Grill 3 minutes; turn. Top each chicken breast half with Muenster cheese slice; continue to grill 2 to 3 minutes or until chicken is no longer pink in center. On bottom half of each roll, layer half the spinach leaves, sprouts and avocado slices. Top each sandwich with grilled chicken breast, half of salsa and top half of roll. *Makes 2 sandwiches*

Grilled Chicken Croissant with Roasted Pepper Dressing

ACKNOWLEDGMENTS

The publisher would like to thank the companies and organizations listed below for the use of their recipes and photographs in this publication.

A.1.® Steak Sauce
BelGioioso® Cheese, Inc.
Birds Eye®
Butterball® Turkey Company
Campbell Soup Company
Colorado Potato Administrative Committee
ConAgra Grocery Products Company
Del Monte Corporation
Delmarva Poultry Industry, Inc.
Dole Food Company, Inc.
The Golden Grain Company®
The HV Company
Kahlúa® Liqueur
Kikkoman International Inc.
The Kingsford Products Company
Kraft Foods Holdings
Lawry's® Foods, Inc.
Lipton®
Holland House® is a registered trademark of Mott's, Inc.
National Chicken Council
National Honey Board
Nestlé USA, Inc.
Newman's Own, Inc.®
Norseland, Inc.
Perdue Farms Incorporated
The Procter & Gamble Company
Reckitt Benckiser
Sargento® Foods Inc.
The Sugar Association, Inc.
Uncle Ben's Inc.
USA Rice Federation
Washington Apple Commission

INDEX

INDEX